DO-IT-YOURSELF
BUSINESS SALES GUIDEBOOK

Do It Yourself
Business Sales Guidebook

**A proven system to help you
sell a business with less than
$1 Million in revenue.**

Ben Brickweg

ISBN: 978-1456568764

Table of Contents

Foreword

Why I created the DIY Business Sales System

As an experienced business transaction professional, I've met with countless business owners that needed to sell, but couldn't afford to pay the standard commission or minimum fee to have a professional advisor help sell their business.

You know what?

I was frustrated, because I knew these small business owners deserved to have useful tools and advice to help them find a buyer for their businesses.

So I rolled up my sleeves and started writing the Do It Yourself

Business Sales Guidebook. I spent over a year compiling and packaging the information learned from my own experiences, mistakes I saw small business owners make, and everything else I could think of that would help folks like you successfully sell their small businesses.

This guidebook will teach you secrets about selling a small business that many owners will never know. The material here is presented in simple and straightforward terms. You'll find 9 modules that give you a step-by-step system for selling your business.

If you have any questions or feedback along the way, please visit us online at www.diybizsales.com and click on the Contact Us link.

Thanks for buying this book.

Ben Brickweg, Author
DIY Business Sales Guidebook

Module 1:
Getting Ready To Sell

Introduction

What's your exit plan?

Can you imagine your life without your business? Many small business owners have never even tried. How about an even more difficult question: can you imagine your *business* without *you*? This doesn't mean for an afternoon while you run to the bank, or a day when you are sick, or even during a month-long vacation. It means forever.

These thoughts should not be frightening. The sweat and tears that you have invested in your business might make it feel like you are inseparable. But even if you and your business are the best of friends, you should try imagining what your exit looks like. What happens if the economy or your health takes a nosedive? Are you ready for the consequences?

The concepts introduced in this book will help you if you are looking to sell your business next week, next year, or next decade. What you can learn here will help you even if you *never plan to sell*. Every small business owner should examine his or her business on a regular basis, figure out what it is worth, and improve its value.

The truth is, many small businesses simply dissolve when the owner can't or doesn't want to continue. It's terrible to see all of your hard work and equity disappear down the drain. So start thinking about your exit now. It doesn't matter how far down the road you imagine it happening.

Why Exit Your Business?

There are many different *reasons* to exit your business, and they may require different exit *strategies*. Be prepared for anything, as you never really know what tomorrow might bring. Here are some of the most common reasons why people like you might want or need to exit their businesses:

- **Retirement:** It's time to cash in and relax, travel, go golfing, watch TV, or whatever else you've envisioned for your golden years.

- **Burnout:** After years of hard work, you just don't feel like doing it anymore.

- **Poor Health:** Bad back, car accident, or frightening diagnosis... these things take us by surprise.

- **Death:** When your time comes, you won't be able to run your business anymore. There's no choice in this case.

- **Divorce:** The judge bangs the gavel and orders you to pay your ex half the value of the family business. It's not likely you have the cash on hand to do so.

- **Children:** You want to pass the business on to the next generation.

- **Inadequate Income:** Family and/or lifestyle changes mean the business isn't providing what you need anymore.

- **Tax and Estate Planning:** With proper planning, you can reduce or defer income tax liability when selling your business.

- **Relocation:** You need to move but can't take the business with you.

- **Partner Conflict:** The relationship isn't working anymore.

- **Debt or Lease Escape:** You need to get out from underneath a substantial liability.

- **Life Happens:** For whatever reason, the time has come to move on.

Do any of these apply to your current situation? Do you expect any of them to be true in the future? You don't need a crystal ball to understand your likely reasons for exiting your business. Think about it so you can plan accordingly.

> ### NOTE
>
> **MANY SMALL BUSINESS OWNERS ATTEMPT TO SELL AND QUICKLY REALIZE THEY SHOULD HAVE MADE SPECIFIC IMPROVEMENTS TO INCREASE THE VALUE OF THEIR BUSINESS BEFORE SELLING. IF YOU CAN, TRY TO DO THESE THINGS *BEFORE* YOU PLAN TO EXIT.**

Ways to Exit

Exactly how you exit your business will depend on your reasons for exiting and several other factors. One of the biggest variables is speed. If you need to get out quickly, your options are limited. You shouldn't expect to sell your business for top dollar in less than six months. A realistic timeframe for selling is one year or more.

You also need to think about what you want out of the exit. Do you need cash proceeds? Do you want to make sure that staff is taken care of if a change in ownership takes place? How much do you care about what happens to the business itself after you leave? How important is it that the business continues in its present form?

Consider your situation very carefully. Talk about it with family, friends, and professional advisors. If you take your time and understand what you need and what, you'll be able to make wise decisions.

For most small business owners, the following list shows the order of possible exit strategies, from most to least desirable.

- Pass it on to children
- Sell it as an operating business
- Close the doors & liquidate
- Declare bankruptcy

This book is all about the second item in that list, but you should understand all of your options. Circumstances may change at any time.

Pass it on to children

This is at the top of the list for many people, but the reality is that only about a third of family businesses are carried on by the second generation, and less than 15 % go on to the third. It can be very difficult to pick a "favorite" child to take over the business.

It is also a challenge to overcome natural generational conflict or accept that your children have a different vision for the business than you. And, as hard as this is to accept, your children might just not want to take over your company.

In many cases, family members don't have the cash to purchase a business. So if you need to benefit financially from your exit, this may not be an option. It's very satisfying to know that your business is being carried on by your children, but you might have to give it away in exchange for this satisfaction.

Even when it is possible, keeping the business in the family requires good planning. It is a process, not an event. It should be a carefully managed transition, not a crisis. Transferring power and transferring assets are complicated activities. Training and timing are also extremely important.

Sell it as an operating business

This is the most attractive option if your exit strategy is about putting as much cash as possible in your pocket. But it's certainly not the *easiest* option. Depending on the type of business and its history of positive cash flow, there's the potential for a great payoff when selling your business. But the process of selling is hard work and a lot of deals die before money even changes hands. You need to do it right, because you usually only get one shot at it.

Timing is critical when selling a business. You need to think about how economic conditions come into play, when leases and other major contracts expire, and how long it will take to prepare the business to sell. You should also remember that successful business sales transactions can take a year or more to complete.

Even if you don't plan on selling your business, it's a good idea to think about what it would take to sell and to make the necessary improvements. Start enhancing the value of your business immediately, so if you do need to sell, or decide to sell, you are prepared.

Here is an overview of some of the important issues in selling a business that you will learn about in this book:

- The preparation process (increasing value, timing, your needs)
- Valuation
- Creating marketing materials
- Finding a buyer
- Structuring a deal
- Financing a deal
- Closing the deal
- Transitioning

Shut the doors & liquidate it

In some cases, liquidation is the only option. Maybe you *have to* get out of your business and don't have the time to sell. Maybe you've tried unsuccessfully to sell. Or maybe the business or industry is in such bad shape that selling is unrealistic. Then cashing in the assets of your business might be the best strategy.

When you liquidate, you list all of your assets, assign a reasonable price to them (fair market value, not book value or purchase price), and look for a buyer. The best-case scenario is when a single buyer purchases the entire package at once. This could be someone that wants your items to use in a similar business. But in most cases, you'll have to sell assets in pieces or call in an auctioneer. These methods usually mean less money for you in the end, but they are quicker and easier.

Liquidation also involves collecting outstanding receivables, paying off debts, tying up contracts and leases, terminating employees, and completing all other legal and financial tasks.

Declare bankruptcy

It's a dirty word, but for some people bankruptcy is the only way to relieve an excessive financial burden. Some business owners simply can't pay off their debts through a sale or liquidation, and servicing those debts will drive them further into the ground after closing down. In this case, bankruptcy may be the best exit strategy.

But think carefully about your future plans and consult with an experienced attorney and accountant. People who treat bankruptcy like an easy escape route without proper planning and advice are sorely disappointed when they find out the hard way that their credit is ruined for many years.

You've just read about the four most common exit strategies. This book is designed to guide you through the selling option. The topics and information, however, will prove useful to any small business owner, regardless of future plans.

> **WARNING**
>
> YOU SHOULD BE VERY TIGHT-LIPPED ABOUT YOUR EXIT STRATEGY. IF EVERYONE KNOWS YOU'RE LOOKING TO SELL, IT MIGHT SABOTAGE YOUR TRANSACTION. EMPLOYEES MAY HEAD FOR THE DOORS. CUSTOMERS OR CLIENTS MAY LOOK ELSEWHERE. THESE CIRCUMSTANCES CAN DAMAGE THE VALUE OF YOUR BUSINESS. BE

PROACTIVE AND CREATE A PLAN FOR WHEN
YOU'LL DISCLOSE YOUR INTENTIONS OF SELLING
TO EMPLOYEES, ADVISORS AND KEY CUSTOMERS.

Who Will Buy Your Business?

Figuring out who might buy your business is an important step. It will help you focus your search, prepare your business, decide on a proper price, and think about possible terms and financing options.

Potential buyers include:

- Family members
- Partners
- Employees
- Strategic buyers
- Private equity groups
- Financial buyers

So far, you've learned a bit about transferring a business to family members. If you're going that route, then some of the information here won't apply to you. The same is true if you have one or more partners who want to exercise their option to buy outlined in your partnership or buy-sell agreement. But the reality is that few partners ever want to pay fair market value for your share of the business.

Selling to one or more employees has certain advantages. They're obviously familiar with the operations and customers, a good transition is much easier, and you could offer ownership in pieces in lieu of salary. But few employees, with all due respect to yours, have enough money or entrepreneurial drive to take over a business. If they did, they would have already started or bought a business instead of working for yours.

Your next option is to move outside your family and business circle. Possible buyers for your business will depend greatly on your company's size and competitive position.

Many small business owners mistakenly believe that their best bet is to find a strategic buyer. A strategic buyer is another business, that wants to purchase your business to enhance their own business and market share. It is quite rare for small businesses, especially in industries like retail, to be acquired by a strategic buyer. It's a little more common in the manufacturing and services industries, but it typically requires a certain minimum in earnings (about $300K / year) and/or valuable intellectual property such as patents and proprietary products.

Another common misperception is that strategic buyers will pay substantially more money for a business than other types of buyers will. However, a strategic buyer is someone who already has know-how and experience, and will usually not pay more than it would cost to create the same advantage from scratch. Strategic buyers don't only evaluate businesses based on earnings potential, but are focused on the value added to their business in terms of assets, market share, or key technologies and systems. So your price really has to make sense.

You might have also heard about Private Equity Groups (PEGs). PEGs are typically looking for businesses with at least $1 million in net income. They will sometimes buy small businesses to bolt onto existing holdings, but chances are that if you're planning a DIY approach to selling your business, you're not in the same league as private equity.

That leaves what are called "financial buyers." This is where most small businesses find success. A financial buyer is a person who wants to own and manage a business which will provide him with a reasonable income. In other words, a financial buyer is probably a lot like you. He or she probably lives in your area or plans to relocate there soon. This buyer is interested in immediate cash flow and an established job. The financial buyer understands that buying a business is less risky than establishing one.

> ## NOTE
>
> THINK ABOUT THE TYPE OF PERSON WHO MIGHT BE IN A SITUATION TO BUY YOUR BUSINESS. IMAGINE A 50-YEAR-OLD EXECUTIVE WHO GETS LAID OFF IN A CORPORATE RESTRUCTURING. IT'S TOUGH FOR HIM TO FIND A JOB SIMPLY BECAUSE COMPANIES CAN HIRE YOUNGER AND CHEAPER. AFTER A FEW MONTHS OF LOOKING FOR A JOB AND WATCHING HIS SAVINGS SLOWLY DISAPPEAR, HE STARTS TO LOOK FOR OTHER OPTIONS. IT MAKES PERFECT SENSE FOR HIM TO *BUY* A JOB FOR HIMSELF. KEEP THIS IN MIND. TO THIS TYPE OF PERSON, CASH FLOW IS IMPORTANT. HE NEEDS A BUSINESS THAT GENERATES $85,000 TO $100,000 IN EARNINGS TO MATCH HIS SALARY EXPECTATIONS.

What are Financial Buyers Looking For?

If financial buyers are, in fact, the most likely buyers of your business, then you need to learn a bit about them. Who are they? What do they want to see in a potential business opportunity?

There are three conditions that every financial buyer wants to satisfy. The financial buyer must be able to:

- Pay himself a reasonable salary
- Service his debt
- Have something left over to grow the business or save for slow months

Of course, different people have different definitions of what a "reasonable" salary is. Just remember that it may not be the same as yours. Regardless, most of a potential buyer's opinion of your business will flow from those three "musts."

Now here is a brief list of what a financial buyer wants to see:

- Historical performance that will likely continue in the future
- Upward trending sales and profits
- Great location
- Favorable lease terms
- Reasonable price
- Equipment and other assets in good condition
- Experienced and well-trained employees

- Relatively easy transition and transferable
client base

On the flipside, there are a number of red flags a financial buyer will be watching out for:

- Large customer concentration
- Business dependence on owner, or chance that relationships won't carry over
- An industry or business trend that has come and gone
- High employee turnover
- A heavy inventory burden
- Obsolete inventory or risk of inventory spoilage
- Declining sales
- Poor record-keeping ("shoebox accounting")
- A high-price, all-cash deal
- High rent payments
- A sales price based on best-case scenarios or wishful thinking

These lists are helpful, but they don't give a complete picture. There are a few other aspects of buyer psychology that you need to understand.

First, money is not always the primary reason a buyer chooses a particular business. Yes, the buyer needs to satisfy certain minimum requirements, but money is usually further down the list in most surveys of small business buyers. Control, freedom, creative opportunities, status, and recognition can all rate higher than money. You must show these benefits to potential buyers. You need to demonstrate the perks of owning a business in general and the fun of owning *your* business in particular.

Second, buyers hate risk, and their strongest emotion is fear. They're afraid of paying too much for a weak business. In your attempts to sell, you should focus on the positives. Potential buyers, however, will be looking at all the negatives, the reasons *not* to buy your business. They will notice all of the little cracks, the cash flow problems, and any other little issues. You need to be prepared for this and ready to reassure the buyer throughout the process.

Of course, there are ways to establish trust, improve buyer confidence and alleviate their worries. You need to be flexible in negotiations. You might provide help in the transition, sticking around for a reasonable training period. Most importantly, you can offer to finance a portion of the sale yourself, which shows you have faith that the business will perform as you are suggesting it will.

Approximately 90% of people who look to buy a business never actually find the right one. For sellers, that means opportunity. There are many potential buyers out there waiting for someone to show them why a particular business is a good investment, not only in terms of money, but also in terms of time and energy. Go convince them that *yours* is their ticket to freedom, a stable salary, and satisfaction.

Learn from Others' Mistakes

You're not the first person to try to sell a small business. Many have tried and failed, and you should learn why. Here's a list of the most common reasons that people *don't* sell their small businesses:

- **The asking price is too high:** remember that buyers are comparison shopping.
- **The asking price is based on the wrong things:** historical performance is the key.
- **The seller refuses to negotiate:** remember the saying "my price, your terms."
- **The seller offers poor terms:** you need to be flexible and accommodate the buyer.
- **The seller is not upfront about the negatives:** potential buyers always find out eventually!
- **The seller neglects the business while selling:** if you don't run the business as usual during the selling process, you can just watch the value disappear.
- **Professional advisors kill a good deal:** picking the wrong advisors that are inexperienced or too risk-averse is a big problem.
- **The business location is bad:** as the saying goes, "location, location, location."
- **The industry is suffering:** there has to be a good history and promising future.
- **The business has poor products, services, or reputation:** this speaks for itself.

- **The business relies on outdated technology or equipment:** you have to keep up with the times.

- **The seller offers a poor transition plan:** buyers need a bit of help learning the ropes.

- **The lease terms are unfavorable:** buyers want stability and security.

- **The seller won't finance the deal:** and if banks won't either, how can a buyer get the cash to buy your business?

- **The seller is slow in communicating or approving qualified buyers:** don't leave good prospects hanging.

- **The business shows poorly:** things have to be clean, organized, and up-to-date.

Assembling a Team

Doing things yourself is great, but you don't have to reinvent the wheel. You'll need help from people who've been involved with the sale of a business before.

At minimum, you'll need a lawyer to help with contracts and an accountant for taxes and financials. Beyond that, your needs will depend on the size and nature of your business. Ask yourself whether you have everything it takes to sell.

- Do you have access to the people who will most likely buy your business?

- How good are you at marketing?

- Are you a skilled negotiator?
- How much extra time do you have?

That last question is extremely important. Remember that selling takes work, and you're going to have to continue running the business *at least* as well as normal while you're trying to sell. If you hate the thought of the hourly charges for a lawyer and accountant, just remember that those people will improve your chances of getting your asking price. They'll also improve your chances of getting a deal done period. 50% of business sales fall apart in the due diligence phase. A good team can prevent this.

The bottom line when it comes to assembling a team is that you select the *right* people for the task at hand. The lawyer who handled your divorce or DUI charge and the accountant who handles your personal tax return may not be the *right* people to handle the sale of your business.

And remember, your team members work for *you*. Pester them with questions. Take the lead. Don't ask them what you should do. Ask them what your options are. *You* are in charge.

NOTE

MANY PROFESSIONALS ARE FEARFUL OF LAWSUITS. AND THEY USUALLY CAN'T BE SUED IF THEY ADVISE YOU *NOT* TO DO A DEAL. PROFESSIONAL GUIDANCE IS IMPORTANT, BUT DON'T LET THEM BLIND YOU TO POSSIBILITIES.

Here's a closer look at the people you might need on your team:

Accountant

The right accountant can help draw up or recast your financials and may have some good ideas about making your business more sellable. He will cooperate with your lawyer to make sure that deals, offers, and financing options make sense.

The right accountant may know the numbers and formulas, but can fail to understand the nuances of the market, the price, and terms that real-world buyers are willing to pay. The right accountant to help you with your sale may or may not be a person that you've relied upon in the past.

Your regular accountant might understand your business, your needs, and you, but he or she may not be ideal for helping you sell your business.

NOTE

AN ACCOUNTANT IS NOT THE SAME AS A BOOKKEEPER. BOOKKEEPERS GENERALLY MANAGE BILLS, CUT CHECKS AND PERFORM ADMINISTRATIVE FINANCIAL DUTIES. ACCOUNTANTS HAVE EXTENSIVE EDUCATION AND TRAINING IN FINANCIAL MATTERS. ACCOUNTANTS WILL HAVE THE "CPA" DESIGNATION.

Lawyer

Having the right lawyer on your team is indispensable when selling a business. He or she will craft and review the legal agreements related to the sale, including the sales contract, closing documents, confidentiality agreements, and seller disclosure statements.

For your convenience, this book provides some sample documents that should be included or used in a transaction, but you need to have an attorney to ensure your documents are comprehensive and right for your precise situation.

The right lawyer for your transaction may not be your regular lawyer. Your regular lawyer may be familiar with your business, your needs, and you, but he or she may be inexperienced in business transactions. For that reason the best lawyer may be an outside specialist.

It's a good idea to interview a few to find the right match. Ask potential lawyers what role they take in a transaction. Just because a lawyer is experienced in drafting documents related to a business transaction, does not mean he has the charisma to keep your deal on track to close. Most worthwhile attorneys won't charge you for an initial meeting to find out if they're a good fit.

Tax advisor

A good tax advisor can provide advice that saves you a lot of money, especially because the sale of your business could launch you into a much higher bracket. A good tax advisor shouldn't step in only after you close a deal; instead, he should help you understand the tax implications of different types of deals and financing options *before* you negotiate with buyers. A good tax advisor can also help you navigate the frustrating hoops set up by the IRS. He or she may or may not be the same person as your lawyer or accountant.

Appraiser

This book will give you an overview of how to figure out the approximate market value of your business. If your situation is complicated or you are very unsure of your valuation, you should hire a professional.

Business appraisers understand the market and where your business fits into the larger picture. A good appraiser does more than just assess the book value of your business.

Broker

Do you need one or not?

The fact that you're reading this means that you suspect the correct answer to that question is no. But they're not all bad and, depending on your situation, they can save you time and money as well as increase your likelihood of selling.

You have to consider economics. A broker will typically charge 10% to 12% or $15,000 to $20,000, whichever is more. For many small business owners, this is simply too expensive.

Oftentimes, if your sales price is under $200,000 and you have the time to devote to conducting the sale on your own, it may not be worthwhile to involve a broker. And in some cases it's not even possible to convince a broker to take you on. You have to be worth *their* time as well.

> ## NOTE
>
> **BROKERS GET PAID OUT OF CLOSING PROCEEDS, NOT AS YOU GET NOTE PAYMENTS ON A SELLER FINANCED DEAL.**
>
> **SALE PRICE IS $100K**
> **DOWN PAYMENT $50K**
> **BROKER FEE $15K**
> **BANK DEBT $30K**
> <u>INCOME TAX ON SALE $20K</u>
> **NET PROCEEDS AT CLOSING: *NEGATIVE $15K***
>
> **A BROKER MIGHT BE COMPLETELY OUT OF THE QUESTION.**

But there are upsides. Involving a good broker can let you focus on running the business while you are trying to sell. A good broker can also provide marketing power and increase the pool of potential buyers. He can guide you through the entire process, handle difficult paperwork, screen potential buyers, and act as a buffer between you and those who might be interested in buying your business.

Because they get paid only if a closing happens, business brokers focus on listings that have a higher chance of selling. If your business is not an "A" listing, there's a good chance a broker won't sell it. But hungry brokers may *take* your listing simply to get the phone to ring. Businesses with profits over $100,000 have a much better chance of successfully selling with a broker than those with earnings under $100,000.

Preparing the Business for Sale

There are several very basic things you should do to make your business more attractive for sale. You don't have to be an expert in buyer psychology to predict some of the things that might enhance your business.

Here are some of the clean-up jobs that you should undertake. Some of them might require a lot of time, so plan ahead and don't put them off until the day you list your business.

Improve or solidify your lease

It's not smart to try selling shortly before a lease expires. Most buyers are interested in stable and secure lease terms, especially if the location is good. Check your lease for a non-assignment clause, which could mean the lease is not transferrable to a new business owner. Some landlords will view a change in ownership as an opportunity to increase rents. You may want to renegotiate your lease before it expires, even if it means accepting a rent increase, just to get terms that will make your business more attractive to buyers.

Review and revise other contracts

Depending on your type of business, you may have supplier contracts, distribution agreements, or other key contracts. Take a close look at these agreements and negotiate to improve them if you can. And make them assignable, if they're not already.

Dispose of outdated, obsolete, or damaged inventory

Assets that a buyer wouldn't want are not really assets. They detract from the overall appeal of your business and may be cluttering storage space, so get rid of them.

Repair or replace outdated or broken equipment

Your business should project a modern and efficient image. Clunky old machinery and yellowing computers don't foster that type of image.

Clean up the books

Shoebox accounting really doesn't cut it when it comes to presenting financial statements to prospective buyers. If your bookkeeping is in need of a major overhaul, you may want to run things for a full year with the new system before trying to sell.

Cut unnecessary expenses

This will help make your business leaner and increase profit margins. Those are major pluses when you try to sell.

Let bad employees go

This requires diplomacy and legal positioning, of course. Not all buyers will want to continue with the same staff, but many will. The transition to a new owner is difficult enough with *good* employees. Potential buyers will not only ask about employees, they'll visit your business and evaluate whether or not they can work with the various people involved.

Make your branding consistent

This means making sure all promotional materials carry the same version of your logo, the look and feel of your website matches your overall image, and every part of your business reflects your core values.

Clean the place up

In many ways, showing a business for sale is the same as

showing a house for sale. Bring in an outsider to give you an honest opinion of the condition of your business. Give the place a new coat of paint and do those little repair jobs that you never got around to. Clean everything inside and out, replace that one dirty ceiling tile in the bathroom, wash the windows, and organize the workspaces.

Finishing Up

There you have it. By now you should understand why you're selling, what you need out of a sale, who might buy your business, and what these people might be looking for. And if you have assembled a good team and done everything you can to make your business appealing, you're ready to move on to the next stage: Preparing Your Financials.

Module 2:
Preparing Your
Financial Documents

Introduction

You've decided that you want to sell your business and made necessary improvements. Now you need to prepare your financials. If you want to get a reasonable price and have buyers take you and your business seriously, you need written proof of your business performance.

This might seem obvious, but your financial statements are extremely important. They will have more influence on the buyer's decision-making process than anything else you do, show, or say during the process of selling your business.

Buyers may be interested in owning their own business for many different reasons, but they need to make a living. If they can't expect to earn a reasonable income from your business, they will look elsewhere. All financial documents should be clean, clear, and professional looking. Projecting the right image is important.

What you Need

If you don't have a good system of bookkeeping or financial tracking, make one now. A filing cabinet stuffed with invoices and bank statements will not sell your business. Remember: clean, clear, and professional.

The basic financial statements that you need are:

- **Profit & Loss (P&L) Statement:** the most important documents of the entire sale, this can also be referred to as an income statement.

- **Recast Profit & Loss Statement:** a document that shows the true earnings of your business. You'll learn more about this in a few pages.

- **Asset List:** a detailed list of the "stuff" in your business

- **Inventory Report:** retail, wholesale, and distribution companies need to know how

much inventory is on hand right now and how
this number fluctuates by season

Supporting documents that you might need down the road in
the due diligence phase are:

- Bank Statements
- Income Tax Returns

Assuming your business has been in operation long enough,
you need to gather a minimum of three years' worth of
financial data. Five years is even better. Only showing your
previous year or another small sample makes buyers
immediately suspicious. They will wonder what you are trying
to hide. Sometimes owners will reduce certain expenses, such
as advertising and development, in the lead-up to a potential
sale. Although this may make a short-term picture look better,
buyers and their accountants will be on the lookout for these
little fixes.

Buyers are looking for trends in the earnings performance of
your business. If that trend is downward, don't even think of
hiding it. It doesn't always make your business undesirable. All
businesses have some problems. Most are solvable if you are
open and honest about them from the beginning. Nearly half of
all deals die in the due diligence phase, and one of the major
reasons is that the financials and contracts did not turn out to
be exactly what the seller represented in the early stages.
Never lie about your financial performance.

What are Earnings?

The realities of small business earnings are nothing like what they teach in business school. As you're well aware, small business owners want to minimize taxes. To do this, they prepare their books and tax returns to show the lowest reasonable net income. The small business owner takes advantage of all sorts of write-offs that make the business appear less profitable than it actually is, so he can keep more of his hard-earned money every year.

NOTE

MIKE'S SPORTING GOODS STORE SHOWS A MERE $40,000 PER YEAR IN NET INCOME ON ITS TAX RETURNS. BUT MIKE DRIVES A LEXUS AND HIS WIFE DRIVES AN AUDI. THEY LIVE IN A FANCY SUBDIVISION WITH DOCTORS AND LAWYERS FOR NEIGHBORS. MIKE'S BUSINESS IS CLEARLY PROVIDING A MUCH BETTER LIFESTYLE THAN THE TAX RETURNS MIGHT INDICATE.

When you look at the true earnings of a business, you want to use a standardized formula to figure out what economic benefits the owner really enjoys. The term for this is *Seller's Discretionary Earnings*, or SDE. That includes not only the net income of the business as shown in the books and claimed to the IRS, but all of the other benefits and perks that have been written off as legitimate business expenses.

The International Business Broker's Association defines SDE as "an estimate of the total financial benefit a full time *owner operator* would derive from the business on an annual basis."

The most common discretionary expenses in small businesses are:

- Interest on any debt the owner carries in the business
- Income taxes paid by the business
- Excess depreciation
- Excessive rent and/or lease payments
- Fair market rent adjustment
- Finance charges / factoring
- Household repairs or services paid for by the company
- Premiums for owner's health, life, and other insurance policies
- Internet service for owner's benefit
- Maid and cleaning services
- Memberships in health clubs, country clubs, etc.
- Non-business shipping and postage costs
- Payroll and employee benefits paid to the owner
- Personal credit cards paid by the business
- Products and services consumed by the owner's family but paid for by the company
- Season tickets
- Any other discretionary expenses that a new owner would not need to cover in order to run the business effectively

Adding these benefits back to the net income is called *recasting* the financial statements. This process helps show a potential buyer the true earning power of your business. The buyer wants to buy your business so he can earn money. Accurately recast financial statements can be his greatest gauge of that possibility.

Remember, the SDE is the yearly net income of the business before the owner pays himself, makes his debt payments, tax payments, interest payments, and any other discretionary expenses that would normally vary from owner to owner.

SDE shows the net benefit to the owner. After all the regular business expenses are covered, what's left? This is what potential buyers want to know.

THE BUYER'S MIND

"I'VE SEEN ALL SORTS OF NUMBER MAGIC THAT TELL ME THIS IS A GOOD BUSINESS, BUT ALL I REALLY WANT TO KNOW IS HOW MUCH THIS GUY TAKES HOME EVERY MONTH."

Recasting Financials/Income Statement

As you've learned, the Profit & Loss Statement is the most important financial document you will present to buyers. You need to recast this in a way that shows potential buyers all of the discretionary earnings available. This shows what the business really generates for a new owner.

For some expenses, you'll have to replace the figures with something reasonable and justifiable. For example, if your daughter was on the payroll for $50K a year but only did cleaning on weekends, you'll have to take that $50K out and add in the realistic cost of a weekend cleaner.

It's not unreasonable to take an aggressive approach to recasting. You really want to show a buyer all of the money that he will have at his disposal if he ends up buying your business. Qualified buyers will understand what you've done. Still, you should make extensive notes and be prepared to explain exactly why you recast things the way you did. Aggressive doesn't mean unrealistic, however. Don't invent new perks to add back, and don't recast things that shouldn't be recast.

WARNING

DON'T LIE ABOUT ANY INCOME OR EXPENSE ITEMS IN YOUR FINANCIAL STATEMENTS. DISCOVERY OF "FUNNY BUSINESS" BY THE BUYER OR HIS TEAM WILL USUALLY BLOW UP YOUR DEAL.

Who Should Prepare Your Statements

Many business owners already have their financial data stored in a computer program. If you do, it will be quick and easy to produce financial statements on your own. If you don't have your data loaded, you will need to do so. You, your bookkeeper, or an accountant can be involved in the process if necessary. The choice depends on the amount of time and money you want to spend and the type of statements you need:

- **Self-prepared statements:** you can simply

print off financial statements from whatever accounting or Point of Sale program you use (e.g. QuickBooks, OWL, Peachtree). An accountant may not have reviewed these, or only at the end of the year to prepare taxes.

- **Compiled statements:** an accountant compiles and organizes information that you provide. The accountant does not test the information for accuracy and won't vouch for the statements.

- **Reviewed statements:** an accountant not only organizes your statements but compares your numbers to industry norms and averages, showing return on equity, profit margins, and other key figures.

- **Audited statements:** an accountant thoroughly examines your statements, counts inventory, and inspects random samples to test for accuracy.

So what type of statements do you need in order to sell your business? Self-prepared statements are most common and usually acceptable. Compiled statements are sometimes done for small business sales, but reviewed statements are rare and audited statements are unnecessary.

The buyer will probably have an accountant working with him, but if your books are up-to-date and clean, you don't really need your own professional to spend any more billable hours working on them.

Nevertheless, involving an accountant will help you address tax issues you may face with the sale of your business. He may be able to lower your taxes enough to completely offset his fees. So just because your books are in good shape doesn't mean you won't need to consult your accountant when selling your business.

What Buyers Look For

The bottom line is the bottom line: how much money does your business make? The single most important question in the buyer's mind is how much he can put in his pocket each month. That makes the Profit & Loss Statement, Seller's Discretionary Earnings, or Income Statement the king of the financial document heap.

But besides the earnings, there are several financial indicators buyers and accountants may be looking at. It's important for you to know what these are and, if necessary, to be able to outline them to a potential buyer.

Gross margins

The gross margin of a product is the difference between sales price and directly related production costs. Basically, it relates to the efficiency with which a business turns materials into goods. For retailers, gross margin indicates mark-up. Buyers may look at the gross margins for each product, watching not only for large gross margins but also for trends. Upward trending is a sign of health. Downward trending may mean a declining product or increased competition.

Accounts receivable

Most small business sales don't include short-term accounts receivable, but a buyer will still want to examine your historic receivables very carefully. Standard payment terms may differ by industry, but buyers will look to see that you have been collecting receivables quickly. If you have trouble collecting from your customers, it will raise concerns, even if the accounts receivable are not included in the sale.

Ratios

There are several different ratios that are important in all industries. These include Return on Equity, Return on Assets, Debt to Equity, and Liquidity Ratio. You can compare these ratios to industry averages to show where your business stands in comparison to others.

Each industry may also have its own commonly used ratios. For example, retail businesses often list "sales volume per square foot." In the food business, you might see "percent of expenses devoted to food costs." Check with your relevant trade association to find out which specific ratios your industry uses.

Outstanding debt

This is generally not included in small business deals because virtually all small businesses are sold free and clear. That means the seller pays all debts at closing and retains all receivables. For businesses priced under $1 million, most buyers will not be interested in buying your debt. Nor will banks lend a buyer any money on an asset that already has a lien. Still, buyers and their advisors might want to see your balance sheet. They are usually looking for signs of trouble like many new loans, steadily increasing balances on loans, or liens that the seller will need to satisfy at the time of closing. You'll want to prepare a list of assets you plan to include in the sale, and it's best to remove damaged or obsolete inventory as well as uncollectable accounts receivable.

What to do About Poor Financial Performance

First and foremost, be 100% honest.

Don't try to hide, obscure, lie about, or otherwise misrepresent poor business performance. It will backfire. Any person with the skills and experience to qualify as a potential buyer will not be fooled. Any deception or misdirection will eventually come out and kill your deal. This might be in the due diligence phase, where 50% of small business deals die. But it might also be *after* the sale, which is potentially worse. If someone buys your business, runs it for a few months or a year, and then finds out that you misrepresented the financial performance, you will certainly get a call from his attorney. Either way, you will needlessly spend time and money, and you have a good chance of losing a subsequent lawsuit.

Remember that a person will purchase your business based on past performance but only with the expectation of future potential. Many potential buyers will see what you've done and feel certain that they can do better. Great! It's much better for the buyer to believe that poor or mediocre performance was due to *your* lack of effort, burn-out, or other personal issues tied to you. If a buyer sees a problem in the industry or economy, or if he thinks that the business and its products are no good and destined for failure, he'll probably stay away.

In the section of this book on writing marketing materials, you will learn more about how to best position weaknesses or performance issues as "growth opportunities". The bottom line is that you should be open about poor performance, outline personal reasons that may have impacted the business, and focus on the future.

THE BUYER'S MIND

"HOW MUCH OF THE PERFORMANCE OF THIS BUSINESS IS RELATED DIRECTLY TO THE CURRENT OWNER/OPERATOR? COULD I DO A BETTER JOB OF IT THAN THIS GUY?"

Other Contracts

An important part of putting together your financials is assembling all of your contracts, reviewing them closely. Where appropriate, consider renegotiating contracts to make them more attractive to prospective buyers. Having good contracts in place can ensure stability for your business and give you a competitive edge.

Contracts include signed and legally binding agreements with:

- Customers/clients
- Suppliers
- Independent contractors
- Strategic partners
- Distributors
- Shipping partners

Once you've assembled all of your contracts, make a comprehensive list spelling out general terms and expiration dates. You should also create a list that doesn't include actual names of suppliers and customers in order to protect confidentiality in the early stages of working with potential buyers.

You need to review these contracts with a mind to making them attractive to buyers. This can involve be difficult because different buyers will view contracts differently. For example, one buyer might see a long-term contract with a supplier as an advantage because it appears to secure a stable source of materials, while another buyer sees the same contract as a disadvantage because he believes he could negotiate better terms with another supplier.

> **HINT**
>
> RUN YOUR BUSINESS AS NORMALLY AS POSSIBLE WHEN YOU ARE IN THE PROCESS OF SELLING. DON'T AVOID RENEWING CONTRACTS, BUYING INVENTORY, OR ANY OTHER REGULAR BUSINESS ACTIVITY. MAKE THE SAME BUSINESS DECISIONS

> **WHEN SELLING AS YOU'D MAKE IF YOU PLANNED ON KEEPING THE BUSINESS FOR MANY YEARS.**

One important feature of a contract is "assignability." An assignable contract is one that may transfer to a new business owner. A non-assignable contract is made with you and you alone.

If a contract is non-assignable, try to make it assignable. Work on other aspects of the contract as well. Negotiate better prices. Lock clearly advantageous contracts into longer terms. Just remember that you need to keep your cards fairly close to your chest. Don't go tell your suppliers and customers that you're preparing to sell. Tell them you're simply looking to improve your business.

Employee & freelancer contracts

Employee and freelancer contracts will be part of your more general package of information outlining your operations. Not all employees will be on contract, of course, but this type of information is essential. Prospective buyers will want to know about the staffing situation. High employee turnover can mean trouble for small businesses.

Equipment leases

Equipment leases may or may not be transferable. You must look into this and decide whether to include such arrangements in the sale of your business. Leasing does offer certain tax benefits, and good leasing terms may improve the appeal of your business. However, buyers may take a negative view of leases that are about to expire. If the remaining term on your equipment lease is a year or less, you should consider paying off the remaining balance at closing. You can then deliver the equipment free and clear of the lease. Plus, if you pay off the lease at closing, you can add back the monthly expense when recasting your financials.

Your Property Lease

A property lease may be the most important contract for any small business. If your business is highly dependent on location, your lease may be your greatest asset. On the other hand, a lease with restrictive and unfavorable terms will prevent buyers from making an offer on your business.

As you read in the section on preparing your business for sale, it can be extremely difficult to sell a business with a looming expiration date on the lease. Just like other contracts, leases can be assignable or non-assignable. If yours is non-assignable and about to expire, any deal will most likely be contingent on the buyer's successful negotiation of a long-term lease with the property owner.

Some things to consider when reviewing your lease:

- Monthly rent
- Assignability
- Length
- Right of first refusal on contiguous space

- Restrictions on business use
- Subletting rights
- Parking
- Safety and insurance
- Advertising restrictions

Don't wait until your lease expires to consider renegotiating. Try to get terms that will appear favorable to prospective buyers. You may have to accept an increase in rent in exchange for more favorable terms or assignability. Some landlords will take advantage of a change in ownership by upping the rent on a space. Buyers know this and will be wary of such situations.

You should assemble and assess all of these contracts and agreements in the preparation phase. Buyers will want information about key contracts early in the selling process, and you have to be ready to answer their questions and provide supporting documents in the later stages.

Module 3:
What's It Worth?

Introduction

What is your business worth?

Most experts will tell you that coming up with a realistic value for a small business is part science and part art. Don't let that intimidate you. It is true there is no universal method of determining the value of a business, but that doesn't mean there's no rhyme or reason to it.

The methods in this book will help you come up with a set of price and terms that will attract prospective buyers and help you sell your business.

If you aren't looking to sell right now, you can certainly use these methods to keep an eye on what your business might be worth as you journey down the path of business ownership.

NOTE

REMEMBER THAT TERMS ARE JUST AS IMPORTANT AS PRICE WHEN SELLING YOUR SMALL BUSINESS. DO YOU THINK SOMEONE INTERESTED IN RUNNING YOUR BUSINESS WILL HAVE ENOUGH IN THE BANK FOR AN ALL-CASH DEAL?

IF YOU ARE SELLING A DRY CLEANING COMPANY FOR $150K, IT'S NOT REALISTIC TO EXPECT TO FIND A BUYER WITH $150K CASH WHO WILL WAKE UP AT 5:30 A.M. AND SPEND 12 HOURS A DAY WORKING IN A HOT DRY CLEANING PLANT.

OFFERING REALISTIC TERMS WILL EXPONENTIALLY EXPAND THE POOL OF BUYERS THAT CAN AFFORD YOUR BUSINESS.

Of course, buyers will have their own methods of valuing your business. Their opinion about price may not be the same as yours. That's fine. You both enter the process of negotiation with a sense of the value, and the final price comes as a result of that process.

In the end, the value of your business is exactly what the best buyer is willing to pay for it. Don't forget that. What *you* think it's worth is important, but if *the buyer* cannot afford your price at your terms, then you are not being realistic.

In general, what are you thinking about when determining your asking price?

- Who is your likely buyer and can he or she afford to buy the business?
- How much cash did your business generate over the past 3 to 5 years?
- What is the likelihood that the earnings will continue for a new owner?
- Are there sufficient hard assets for bank financing to be available?
- Do the financial statements show sufficient net income for bank financing?
- What do similar businesses sell for?
- Do you need to pay a business broker from your proceeds?
- Can you afford to sell now or do you need to spend time increasing the value?

Notice that this list does not include anything about your emotional attachment to the business or how long and hard you have worked.

NOTE

YOUR "BLOOD, SWEAT AND TEARS" ARE VALUABLE ONLY IF THEY INCREASED THE PROFITS OF THE BUSINESS.

This leads us to a couple of common mistakes when pricing a business for sale:

- **The price is based on future potential.** You can't say to the buyer: "Really, if you changed this, and did that differently, and tried doing this, business would boom!" Put yourself in the buyer's shoes, and ask yourself: "So why didn't the seller do that?" Historical performance is a much more important indicator than future potential. Buyers will buy because of potential, but they will pay based on historical earnings.

- **The price is based on the seller's needs rather than performance.** This does not mean that your needs aren't important. But just because you owe the bank $100,000 and you need $400,000 to retire doesn't mean a buyer is going to pay half a million dollars for your business.

- **The price is not in line with comparable businesses for sale.** Your price needs to be justifiable. If you're asking $200,000 for your business and a buyer sees similar businesses for $40,000, that buyer will dismiss your business as overpriced and he won't come back.

Buyers are smart. They're looking to make an enormous investment and they'll arrive with their homework complete. Be careful not to "burn buyers" by seeking unreasonable price and terms.

Once a buyer labels your business a dud, you'll have a tremendously difficult time getting him to take another serious look.

> **THE BUYER'S MIND**
>
> **"IF I BUY THIS BUSINESS, I WILL NEED TO SERVICE THE DEBT, PAY MYSELF A DECENT SALARY, AND PUT THE EXTRA TOWARD GROWING THE BUSINESS. DOES PAYING THIS PRICE ALLOW ME TO DO THAT?"**

So, how do you determine your asking price? There are many value models, some simple and some extremely complex. Sure you can pay a valuation professional thousands of dollars for a formal valuation. Formal valuations may be analytically and factually correct, but they can be useless when figuring out what a real buyer will pay.

When selling a small business, there are simple approaches to determining price and terms that will help you get the most value and have the best chance of closing a deal.

Overview of Small Business Value Methods

There are two basic types of value methods explained in this guidebook: asset based and multiple of earnings. You may have also heard about market based valuation, discounted cash flow, excess earnings, or other types of valuations. These methods all have various pros and cons, but the reality is they are usually overkill when figuring out what the market will pay for your small business.

Remember that price might seem like the most important thing, but the terms you offer are what will get a deal done. And your price may depend on what those terms look like. Prepare to be flexible. Build in some room for negotiation.

> **NOTE**
>
> HAVE YOU HEARD THE SAYING "YOUR PRICE, MY TERMS?" WELL, IT RINGS TRUE IN BUSINESS SALES. YOU MAY NOT GET ABSOLUTELY EVERYTHING YOU WANT. THE SALE OF A BUSINESS IS THE RESULT OF A DIFFICULT NEGOTIATION PROCESS.

Asset based value

What's your "stuff" worth?

or

The sum total of the business assets equals price.

In this case, price is *not* based on performance. This type of valuation typically generates a lower price than other methods.

So why would you use it? Well, if your business is new, it's hard to assess the value based on performance. Or if your business has been losing money, performance based methods may result in a disappointingly low figure. And if you need to sell quickly, for whatever reason, liquidating your assets may be your only option.

An asset based value involves listing all of your assets, deciding on their fair market value, and adding the numbers together to get a total value. Even if you don't intend to use an asset based value to determine an asking price, it's a good idea to do this analysis. One, it will give you an idea of the low end value of your business. Two, buyers will want to know exactly what they're getting if they end up buying your business and you'll want to have a list to show them.

> **CAUTION**
>
> FAIR MARKET VALUE IS **NOT** WHAT IT COST YOU
> TO BUY YOUR ASSETS, NOR IS IT THE BOOK VALUE
> SHOWN ON YOUR BALANCE SHEET. FOR A QUICK
> ANALYSIS OF THE FAIR MARKET VALUE OF YOUR
> ASSETS, LOOK UP SIMILAR ITEMS FOR SALE ON
> WEBSITES SUCH AS EBAY OR CRAIGSLIST.

One thing to note about selling the assets of your business is that buyers may want to pick and choose items they want and negotiate individual prices. A buyer might look at your list of assets and say "Oh, I already have three computers that I'll be using so I don't need those... and I really don't want all of the desks..." As for dollar values, make sure they are realistic. Remember: fair market value. If a buyer can get something new for close to the price that you're asking for your used items, then he'll probably reject your prices.

Multiple of earnings value

What's the value of your company's ongoing
ability to make money?

or

Earnings times a certain multiple equals price.

In this approach, the performance of your business determines the price. It makes a lot of sense. Someone will buy your business if they think they can earn money from it, and the more money they can earn, the more they'll be willing to pay.

This generally gives your business a higher price than an asset based value, since it wraps up goodwill and future earning potential into your value. Small business buyers usually feel more comfortable buying an existing business with a proven track record of success, instead of buying equipment and inventory to start from scratch.

Everything your business does well - the hard-won loyalty of your regular customers, your proven products and services, excellent location with a favorable lease, all of your fabulous ideas, staff that you've trained and taken care of - are reflected in profits.

"Earnings times a certain multiple equals price" is the simple version. A little later in this module you'll learn *which* earnings and *which* multiple to use.

Which approach should you use?

Although a multiple of earnings approach can give a higher business value, there are a couple of important things to remember.

First, if you need to sell your business quickly, the higher price of a multiple of earnings value may not be the way to go. You have to be willing to go out and find multiple prospective buyers in order to find one with the skills, ability, cash and motivation to purchase your business.

Second, this multiple of earnings approach is highly dependent on the terms you offer. What someone can and will pay your business depends on how much cash he has to pay upfront, how much help you can offer post-sale, whether current staff will stay on with the new owner, whether you'll offer a non-compete agreement, and a wide range of other factors.

Bottom line: if you need to sell quickly, don't have a verifiable history of positive cash flow, or don't have the time and energy to find the "right" buyer for your business, you may have to sell based on your fair market asset value.

Asset Based Value

What are the parts of your business worth?

Calculating the asset based value is a good idea regardless of whether it is used to determine your asking price. You can compare it with a multiple of earnings value. If the asset based value is higher than the multiple of earnings value, it means the parts of your business are worth more than the business itself, based on earning potential. In that case, the asset based value may determine your price.

On a basic level, an asset based value involves listing everything your business has and assigning a dollar value to it. To do this we need to differentiate between tangible and intangible assets. Tangible assets are ones you can touch, like equipment, while intangibles are those you can't, like patents.

Tangible Assets

Your tangible assets include furniture, fixtures, equipment, vehicles, real estate, inventory, and all the other "stuff" in your business.

NOTE

In most small business sales the seller will retain cash, cash equivalents and accounts receivable/payable.

Create a list. To make it easier for you and prospective buyers, choose a way of categorizing your assets. This could be by type (computer equipment, furniture, office supplies, etc.) or location (reception, storage room, manager's office, etc.).

Beside each item, list the date it was purchased and the purchase price. In a fourth column, list the item's fair market value. This is the price that you could get for the item if you tried to sell it. This may require some research on eBay, craigslist, or other websites such as those of used equipment distributors. In a fifth column, you can make notes about the item and your reasons for valuing it the way you did. This may help you once you get into the nitty-gritty of an asset sale, when the buyer is arguing over the price of individual items.

NOTE

You may see lists of assets with values determined by Book Value, which is essentially purchase price less depreciation. Standard depreciation is normally calculated as a percent per year, often 20%. This results in a value that is usually higher – in some cases much higher – than the fair market value. Would you pay $800 for a computer that someone bought last year for $1,000? Probably not. Stick with fair market value.

For inventory, you should start by removing slow-moving items that are completely obsolete. Although these may have some value, they will actually detract from the overall impression of business health. Unless you think prices have changed drastically, you should value inventory at your actual cost.

There you have it. The total of all these items is the value of your tangible assets. Depending on your situation, you can expect a buyer to be willing to pay 60-90% of this value. The likely sales price is lower if you need to sell quickly, if you use values on the high side of reasonable for your assets, or if the buyer will need to spend money to make your business profitable.

Intangible Assets

Intangible assets are the things we can't touch. There are a few different types of intangible assets, and they are notoriously difficult to value. If your asset based value is going to include this type of asset, you may want to consult an accountant with experience in the field.

Some of the different types of intangible assets are listed below:

- Intellectual property, including trademarks, patents, copyright, and licensing agreements
- Software, websites, and marketing collateral
- Customer lists, databases, and historical sales reports

- Goodwill, including your company's brand equity, reputation, recognition, edge over your competitors, specific ways of doing things, your staff's expertise, and industry knowledge

Although we can't touch these things, they certainly have value. Do your best to put price tags on these intangible assets. Do some research to find out how they've been valued in similar circumstances. You can also find online checklists and questionnaires to determine how powerful your brand name is.

For some intangible assets, you can use an approach similar to the one discussed for tangible assets. If you had a website created in the last three years or so, look up what it cost you to have it created. Take this number and cut it in half and add it to your asset value worksheet. This can also work for software or marketing collateral, but only if they are recent. The value for outdated material is next to nothing.

Generally, small businesses don't hold much value in their intellectual property. Trademarked or copyrighted logos and marketing materials aren't worth much to most buyers. If you happen to have a patent, you should consult a professional to see what its value may be. Distribution or licensing agreements usually only have a value if they are transferrable and difficult to obtain.

In some jurisdictions, liquor licenses are both limited and transferrable, giving them a unique value in the open market. In this case, contact a local business owner or professional to find out what the true value may be.

One intangible asset that is especially difficult to value is goodwill. What is goodwill? It's the synergy that your tangible and intangible assets produce. It is your reputation, brand recognition, respect, and customer base all wrapped up in one. In asset based value models, goodwill usually isn't listed separately. Logically, if a business has valuable goodwill, it will earn more money. To the extent that your goodwill has value, it will be better reflected in a multiple of earnings value model. If you aren't able to use a multiple of earnings model, then your goodwill probably doesn't have much value to most buyers.

So, what do you do with an asset based value? It really depends. Sometimes you can run a multiple of earnings valuation and find it comes up with a lower value than your asset based value. This is probably because you don't earn much money. In this case, you'll want to use the asset value as your asking price. If you need a very quick sale, then you might be looking for someone who simply wants to purchase your tangible assets. This value can also be useful when allocating the sales price for tax planning purposes.

Multiple of Earnings Value

What is the value of your business based on its ability to generate profit?

Unlike an asset based value, which measures what your business *has*, a multiple of earnings model measures what your business can *do*. Most buyers are more interested in the profits that your business assets generate than the assets themselves.

Because the multiple of earnings model bases the business value on performance, it may not be the way to go if your business is new or performs poorly. Still, it can be helpful to compare these results with those of other methods.

The idea is fairly simple:

Earnings x   multiplier   =   value of your business

Great. Now you need to look a little closer at those first two items. What exactly are "earnings" and what "multiplier" do you choose?

Earnings

Use the Seller's Discretionary Earnings, or SDE, that you calculated in Module 2.

Remember, the SDE is the yearly net income of the business before the owner pays himself, makes his debt payments, tax payments, interest payments, and any other discretionary expenses that would normally vary from owner to owner.

SDE shows the net benefit to the owner. After all the regular business expenses are covered, what's left? This is what potential buyers want to know.

What SDE figure should you plug into the formula? In most cases, you should take the average of your last three years. This will present a fair and accurate picture. Using only the past year might give you a higher price, but it can make you lose credibility with the buyer. Be honest with yourself. If you had an abnormally bad year last year, you would certainly factor in previous years to show the real picture of the business. So do the same thing if the most recent year was abnormally good. If business has been trending steadily upward, you can weight the past three years differently, 60% - 30% - 10%, for example. Whatever the case, you must be reasonable in how you arrived at your price. Anything less than full disclosure will make buyers suspicious.

What about basing it on other "earnings?" A few are outlined here, though SDE is generally recommended as the most accurate representation of small business value to potential buyers.

- **Earnings Before Interest and Taxes (EBIT):** may be useful for larger businesses sold to an investor who will hire another person to run the business
- **Sales:** sometimes used in the service industry, particularly restaurants, but it still doesn't address buyers' primary concern, which is profit
- **Future Earnings:** may enhance value if business has been trending upward, but the future is extremely hard to predict and a valuation based on future earnings appears riskier to buyers

Multiplier

For small businesses, the proper multiplier is usually between 2 and 3, but it can be as low as 1 or as high as 5.

The value multiplier is the greatest point of discussion and contention in business value. Don't let that scare you. The exact multiplier is going to fall within a certain range based on your industry and be fine-tuned within that range according to things that add or detract from the value of your business.

Let's begin with a general look. Remember that this depends greatly on performance:

	Low to mid (1 to 3)	Mid to high (2.5 to 5)
Characteristics	* Higher risk * Earnings under $150k /year * Not asset or equipment intensive * Customers loyal to particular owner/operator	* Lower risk * Earnings over $150k /year * Asset or equipment intensive * Diverse and established customer base
Examples	* Service Industry (hair salons, accountants, daycares) * Retail Industry	* Manufacturing * Distribution

Market Based Value

What you really need is a starting point. The table above will give you a general range, but within that range where do you start?

The best answer comes from the sales of comparable businesses. Market based value is standard in the real estate business, partly because realtors have access to thousands of listings and can make comparisons quite easily. In business sales, this kind of information has traditionally been a bit more difficult to access. With the Internet, however, things have become easier. You can go online and search for ads for similar businesses in similar industries and markets. You can also contact a business broker and industry associations to find out what is happening in your area.

On the Internet, view other listings to make sure you're not way out of line. Let these be your starting points, and adjust according to your specific situation. You can bet that potential buyers are comparison shopping, so you'd better prepare yourself with the same information.

THE BUYER'S MIND

"I SEE THAT THERE ARE A FEW OTHER PET STORES LISTED FOR $200,000, AND THIS ONE EARNS ABOUT THE SAME, HAS BEEN AROUND LONGER, AND IS IN A BETTER SUBURB... SO IT SHOULD BE WORTH AT LEAST $200,000."

In a market economy, these kinds of comparisons have a powerful logic. Your accountant may have burnt out his calculator in coming up with a complex valuation, but if it doesn't match anything happening in the real world, how useful is it?

Value Drivers

The multiple you use, and the value of your business, is going to adjust up or down according to several factors called "value drivers." Examples of value drivers include the number of years you've been in business, your competitive edge, your lease terms, your customer base, how well your business will transition to a new owner, your location, and your sales trends. These types of factors must be accounted for. Value drivers can help you determine the exact multiple to use within the acceptable range for your industry.

In a business sale, the seller tends to focus on the positive value drivers, while the buyer focuses on the negative value drivers. Don't worry. Every business has some negative aspects. It doesn't mean the business is a dud. In fact, wouldn't you worry as a buyer if there appeared to be absolutely *nothing* wrong with a business?

The real issue is what you do about negative value drivers. Your first option is to fix what's broken. This may be as simple as getting rid of outdated inventory or cutting back on staffing during non-peak hours. It may also mean waiting to sell. You might want to spend a year or more increasing the value of your business. Your second option is to be completely open about the negatives and to adjust the price accordingly. You can explain to buyers what you've done in your pricing and why. Your third option is to let the buyer figure out the negatives for himself.

By using a multiple of earnings model based on your industry's rules of thumb adjusted for value drivers and comparable business sales, you should be able to arrive at a reasonable price for your business. Remember you're determining an *asking* price. The final price is arrived at through the negotiation process. If anything, negotiation will result in a price reduction, so start off at the high side of reasonable. Your final selling price is also highly dependent on terms. If the terms are right, a buyer may end up accepting a price he first thought to be too high.

If you're having trouble, or you want confirmation on your price, you may want to consult a broker or pay for a professional valuation.

> **CAUTION**
>
> **BEWARE OF EXPENSIVE VALUATIONS.**
>
> **A PRICEY VALUATION MAY USE METHODS THAT ARE MORE APPROPRIATE FOR LARGER BUSINESSES THAN YOURS. YOU NEED A VALUATION THAT ACCOUNTS FOR SMALL BUSINESS REALITIES, LIKE THE FACT THAT THE NEW OWNER WILL NEED TO HAVE ENOUGH AFTER PURCHASE TO PAY HIMSELF, SERVICE HIS DEBT, AND GROW THE BUSINESS.**
>
> **A SMALL BUSINESS VALUATION SHOULD COST BETWEEN $5 AND $10 THOUSAND. IT SHOULD NOT COST BETWEEN $20 AND $50 THOUSAND, AS SOME WILY FIRMS WILL TRY CHARGING.**

In the end, you shouldn't forget that a) your business is worth only as much as a willing buyer will pay, and b) the terms of a deal are as important as the price, if not more important.

Seller Financing

Let's be realistic: *Would a guy with enough money to pay all cash for your business really want to run your business every day?* The saying among business brokers is that guys with the wealth to pay cash for businesses have bad knees and backs, and they certainly won't want to work long hours or get their hands dirty. They'd also be wiser to leverage that cash in a larger business and make more money for themselves.

Depending on your price, chances are slim to none that you're going to get an all-cash deal. If you do insist on all cash, be ready to discount your price by 30-50% and double the time you spend looking for a buyer.

Banks really don't like to lend for small business purchases
Some sort of financing is inevitable when selling a small business. But banks are very reluctant to finance business sales when a large part of the price is goodwill and when there aren't hard assets to repossess if the buyer defaults on the loan. Plus, small business financial statements often show as little profit as possible for tax purposes. Those tax returns don't impress bankers. Banks also want to see a lot of collateral and buyers with a combination of specific industry experience and high net worth. And the bank financing process is long and complicated.

So what can an eager seller and buyer do?
Seller financing is the obvious, and best, solution. In fact, about 80% of all business sales involve some form of seller financing. Another 10% are all cash transactions, while the last 10% involve bank financing. These figures underline what most business brokers have already learned and recommend.

NOTE

REMEMBER THE THREE RIGHTS OF SELLER FINANCING: YOU CAN'T TAKE A RISK ON JUST ANYBODY. WHEN FINANCING A BUYER, IT'S VERY IMPORTANT FOR YOU TO FIND THE *RIGHT* BUYER, WITH THE *RIGHT* DOWN PAYMENT AND THE *RIGHT* SECURITY.

Benefits of seller financing

Why exactly should you consider seller financing?

- **Get more money:** You're more likely to get something close to your asking price, and charging interest increases your overall return.

- **Increase the buyer pool:** Because you're not asking for everything upfront, you increase exponentially the number of people who are capable of buying your business. That increases your chances of success.

- **Lower your tax burden:** An all cash deal may mean a higher tax rate in the year you sell. Spreading your earnings out over several years can mean spreading out the tax burden and saving money. Consult your attorney or CPA for an analysis of tax consequences.

- **Close a deal faster and easier:** Even if a buyer's bank *is* willing to finance a deal, it's going to set up some hoops to jump through. Those hoops will stretch the process. And if you've heard that the Small Business Administration can help out by guaranteeing loans, don't get too excited. It is difficult to qualify, and the process is lengthy and cumbersome.

- **Establish trust with buyers**: For the seller, financing the deal means you're sharing the buyer's risk. It shows you're confident the business will perform like you've promised it will. From the buyer's perspective, it's a form of guarantee.

And the drawbacks? The primary drawback of offering seller financing is that you are taking on the risk of default. You're betting on the buyer's ability to run the business well, turn a profit, and pay you what he or she owes. Fortunately, there are ways to minimize that risk and to protect yourself in case of failure (see "Protecting Yourself").

Basic Terms

Down payment

Aim for 1 to 1.25 times the Seller's Discretionary Earnings, or 30% to 50% of the asking price.

Typically, the higher the sale price, the larger the dollar amount you will be financing. That means you earn more through interest payments. However, the more the buyer puts down, the more he has at stake in the business and the harder he'll work to make it successful. A larger down payment will also reduce the buyer's monthly payments, which is important to both of you because servicing a larger debt increases risk.

Remember that the down payment has to cover your expenses related to the sale. These include fees (appraiser, lawyer, accountant, broker), taxes (sales, capital gains, depreciation recapture, personal and corporate income tax) and paying off any debts the buyer does not assume.

At the same time, be careful you don't leave a buyer cash-strapped. He will also have expenses related to the transaction. He will need enough money for living and operating once the takeover is complete. Even very healthy businesses may experience a drop in sales and/or profits in the post-sale period. The buyer needs to be financially prepared for that. If the buyer has fronted all of his available cash, he may find it difficult to make the monthly payments. That's a situation you don't want, so be realistic, even if the buyer isn't.

> ## NOTE
>
> THE RIGHT DOWN PAYMENT WILL VARY BY BUYER. IT'S IMPORTANT TO FIND A BUYER WITH THE SKILL, EXPERIENCE, AND KNOWLEDGE TO BE SUCCESSFUL IN YOUR BUSINESS. THEN MAKE SURE YOU GET A HIGH ENOUGH PERCENTAGE OF HIS NET WORTH AS DOWN PAYMENT TO MAKE SURE HE CAN'T AFFORD TO WALK AWAY, BUT NOT SO MUCH THAT A FEW BAD MONTHS WILL MAKE HIM RUN OUT OF CASH.

You may even want to find out where the buyer is getting his down payment from. Is it coming from his savings? Or is a family member helping out? If he's getting help, then he may be financing the *entire* purchase and wind up with two monthly payments to make. You need to feel confident he can successfully service his entire debt while running the business.

Interest

Shoot for 6% to 9%.

According to many brokers, business buyers are not only willing to pay for seller financing, they're willing to pay more than the bank rate. That's great news for you. If you're collecting interest, you could get substantially more than your sales price from the sale of your business.

In fact, the equivalent Return-On-Investment can be higher than you'd expect on other types of investment.

With seller financing, you can make the interest rate the focus of the negotiation. If a prospective buyer doesn't like your asking price, you can offer to move a bit on the interest rate in exchange for keeping the price where it is. Understand that this means you shouldn't start too low on the interest rate.

Interest adds up fairly quickly, as you probably know if you've been carrying a mortgage or another large loan. This time, *you* benefit. Consider a simple scenario: you sell your business for $100,000. The buyer gives you 50% in cash and finances the remaining $50,000 with you. You agree to a 7.5% interest rate over 5 years. The total repaid will be $60,114. Your interest earnings are just over 20% of the principal.

Repayment Period
Consider 3 to 5 years.

Again, you're balancing your risk with concern for the buyer's ability to be successful in running your business. You don't want to stretch the amortization period too long because you will be increasing the duration of your risk. The buyer might, despite your due diligence, turn out to be a poor business owner. Or the economic climate might change a few years down the road.

But remember, you don't want a rapid repayment plan to burden the buyer with large monthly payments that make it difficult for him to service his other debts, pay himself, and build the business. You have a stake in the buyer's success, and you should design the terms to improve his chances.

Sometimes you need to stretch the payment term to make the cash flow work. If so, make sure to structure your loan with a final balloon payment after about 60 months. This reduces the amount the buyer pays back on a monthly basis and gives him a fighting chance to grow the business.

Consider this scenario: with that $50,000 financed over 5 years at 7.5% interest with a final balloon of $20,000, the buyer's monthly payments are reduced by almost 30% while your total proceeds go up to $63,671. Your interest earnings are just over 27% of the principal.

Protecting yourself

Yes, seller financing comes with risk.

If the buyer can't successfully run your business long enough to pay you off, you don't get your money. But there are ways to protect yourself, to minimize the risk, and to increase the buyer's chance of success. And remember, if the buyer defaults and you get the business back, you get to keep the original down payment.

Find the Right Buyer

Perform due diligence on the buyer. When you've got a prospective buyer, do a credit check and assess his personal financial statement and assets. Is he financially capable? You're not just looking for someone who can afford to *buy* your business, you're looking for someone who has the ability to *run* it. Look at the buyer's work experience, past success or failure in business, and personal references.

Imagine you're hiring a president or manager. Does the buyer have the right personal and professional capabilities? Remember, you're the banker lending him money, so don't be afraid to ask questions and check references.

Structure the Right Deal
The right deal minimizes your risk and maximizes the buyer's stake.

You minimize your risk by not loaning too much and avoiding a lengthy amortization period. You maximize the buyer's stake by requiring a significant down payment.

The right deal also has reasonable and realistic repayment terms. Don't burden the buyer with high monthly payments. Remember that he's not only paying you, he's paying himself. Also realize that the buyer will probably be faced with reduced profits in the weeks immediately following the sale. He might have a difficult learning curve, and some of the business's customers may not like the change of ownership.

Make Sure Things are on the Right Track
Keep an eye on your investment. Make sure the buyer provides monthly financial statements as well as annual tax returns. You can also demand the right to visit the business premises with 24 hours notification. These measures will allow you to spot problems before they happen and to prevent unwanted surprises.

NOTE

IF YOUR BUSINESS LEASES SPACE, KEEP YOUR NAME ON THE LEASE.

THIS MAY SEEM COUNTER-INTUITIVE, BUT IT HELPS YOU KEEP AN EYE ON THINGS. ONE OF THE FIRST SIGNS OF TROUBLE IS MISSED RENT PAYMENTS. IF YOUR NAME IS ON THE LEASE, THE LANDLORD WILL NOTIFY YOU OF LATE RENT, EVEN IF THE BUYER IS TOO PROUD TO LET YOU KNOW. PLUS IF YOU HAVE TO TAKE THE BUSINESS BACK, YOU WILL STILL HAVE LEGAL RIGHT TO THE PROPERTY AND CAN TAKE OVER VERY QUICKLY.

Deal with problems right away. Protecting your investment means watching that the buyer complies with the terms of the deal. Make sure the buyer understands the consequences of default, and make sure you're prepared to follow through on such consequences. At the same time, you might want to help the buyer through rough spots. You are very familiar with the business and the market, and that knowledge and experience might improve the buyer's chances of success. But don't feel you have to be Mr. Nice Guy. If your debtor isn't holding up his end of the bargain, you need to take action.

HINT

MOST BUYERS UNDERESTIMATE THE AMOUNT OF CASH THEY'LL NEED TO CARRY THEMSELVES THROUGH THE FIRST YEAR AFTER BUYING YOUR BUSINESS.

THEY ALSO OVERESTIMATE THEIR ABILITY TO INCREASE PROFITS. THE LESSON? BE REALISTIC EVEN IF THE BUYER IS NOT.

And finally, you can pay for good protection. Your attorney can minimize your risk and draft legal documents that protect you in the event that the buyer fails to pay.

Module 4:
Creating Marketing
Materials

Introduction

After you've determined a realistic price for your business, but before you start looking for potential buyers, you need to create marketing materials. More importantly, you need to create *compelling* marketing materials.

First impressions are important, so marketing materials have to be well-written, professional, and appealing. Take your time. Give it careful thought. Hire someone to help if necessary. Definitely get at least one other pair of eyes to review and proofread what you've created.

Taking the time to develop comprehensive and convincing business profiles will not only attract buyers, but will actually help you refine your sales pitch. It will prepare you to sit down with a buyer and explain your business's strengths and growth opportunities. It will also help you identify the key features or selling points of your business.

At this stage, there are two important pieces to your marketing materials: the Blind Profile and the Confidential Business Profile, or CBP. The Blind Profile gives potential buyers a tangible, attention-grabbing, preview of your business. It provides just enough information to make them want to proceed to the next step. If the buyer signs a confidentiality agreement, he may receive the Confidential Business Profile. This profile is more comprehensive, covering all the important details of your business and operations. Buyers will refer back to this document throughout the process.

Your business profiles are more than just facts. They have to present a convincing sales pitch and address what you believe will be potential buyers' primary concerns or fears about your business. At the same time, your profile doesn't reveal everything. It should provoke curiosity while answering a buyer's major questions.

In the selling process, a buyer will receive a Blind Profile before a Confidential Business Profile, but you should write these documents in the opposite order. Start with the comprehensive Confidential Business Profile and then you can boil it down into a tight and effective Blind Profile.

Why Confidentiality is So Important

It is essential to have any prospective buyer sign a confidentiality or non-disclosure agreement before seeing your CBP. Never feel uncomfortable asking someone to do this. It is standard procedure. Anyone who doesn't like the idea should be avoided. Make sure your accountant and other members of your team understand that the potential sale of your business is confidential and ask if they are willing to sign a confidentiality document as well. Your lawyer can provide you with a document sufficient to protect your interests in accordance with local laws.

Why all the fuss about confidentiality? Simply put, you don't want the general public to know you're selling your business. Employees and customers may become concerned about what kind of change lies ahead. This will affect their behavior, usually for the worse. They might abandon you altogether. If your competitors know you're trying to sell, they may use it against you. They may encourage the spread of your news and wait for your self-destruction. These are things you don't want to happen at any time, but they're especially damaging when you're trying to sell.

Good buyers will understand that a lack of secrecy will damage the value of a business. So if you *don't* ask a buyer to sign a confidentiality agreement, it might raise alarms about you.

THE BUYER'S MIND

"THIS GUY DIDN'T ASK ME TO SIGN A CONFIDENTIALITY AGREEMENT. HE JUST HANDED ME HIS PROFILE! BAD NEWS. EVERYBODY MUST KNOW THAT HE'S SELLING. THIS BUSINESS IS DEFINITELY OFF MY SHORTLIST."

Confidentiality is a two-way street. To qualify potential buyers, you will be asking them for some sensitive information. They will be revealing details of their experience, background, and financial means. You must protect this information carefully.

The Confidential Business Profile (CBP)

The confidential business profile is a detailed description of your business, written with prospective buyers in mind. It should highlight your strengths without hiding your weaknesses and generate excitement about your business. It is impossible to overstate the importance of this document. It must be well-written and attractive.

If you don't feel confident writing and designing it yourself, have someone help you with it.

> **WARNING**
>
> DO *NOT* PROVIDE FINANCIAL PROJECTIONS.
> FORECASTING PERFORMANCE IS A TRICKY
> BUSINESS AND YOU MAY FIND YOURSELF IN LEGAL
> TROUBLE IF YOU SELL THE BUSINESS TO SOMEONE
> WHO CAN SHOW THAT YOU GAVE FALSE
> EXPECTATIONS.

Sections of the CBP

Company Overview and History

This section briefly outlines the history of the company. It also gives information about the founders, the founding vision, company growth, business structure, and the current ownership. It is the "story" of your business. Describe the strengths of your business. You might highlight competitive advantages, accolades and awards, growth opportunities, exclusive contracts, proprietary rights (without being too specific), key staff members or managers, or anything else you see as a particularly attractive point.

Product and/or Service Overview

Buyers will certainly want to know what products you sell or what services you provide. Give a detailed explanation so buyers understand the value you provide to customers. Make sure to mention top selling items and any seasonality.

Business Strengths

In this section, you should outline some of the strengths of your business. This could mean having a loyal customer base, enjoying exclusive product or regional rights, having a location with a lot of foot traffic, maintaining low overhead, or having a strong Internet presence. You can list these factors in table form and provide notes on how your business demonstrates these strengths.

Growth Opportunities

Here is where you point out how the business can grow in the future. Be very careful not to make unrealistic predictions, but suggest promising areas of development. Perhaps the time is ripe for expansion into a new territory, or there is a new industry trend that the business is well-positioned to compete in. Explain why the future is bright for the industry in general and your business in particular.

Location and Facility Summary

Provide basic information including address, square footage, and leasing costs. If you own the building or property used by the business, make sure you mention whether or not it is included in the business sale. Point out any key advantages to your location.

Employee Information

The employee chart is a graphic representation of the staffing of your business. It should show the hierarchy of your personnel at a glance. It should be a simple description of staff members, their hourly rate, hours worked per week, and tenure.

Competitor & Industry Information

Here is where you outline important information about the general industry in which your business operates and the competition in the market. You should describe how the industry differs from other industries in terms of capital and labor intensity, technology and systems requirements, gross margins, advertising, and distribution. Highlight the strengths of your business in comparison with competitors.

Transition

Tell prospective buyers what you are willing to do, and unwilling to do, to help a new owner learn the ropes. This may mean a formal training period in which you are on site with the new owner and/or a period during which you are available to help as a consultant.

Price and Terms

The proposed deal structure includes your price and the reasons for that price. Point out why your valuation is conservative. Mention what the sale does and doesn't include. Outline financing terms and minimum requirements to qualify as a buyer. Also mention any other important terms of an agreement, such as your willingness to enter a non-compete agreement. Make sure you don't appear inflexible. State that you are open to negotiating exact details of the terms with qualified buyers.

Financial Summary

The financial summary should include a chart of previous years' earnings (minimum three, ideally five). It can also contain key figures such as cost of sales, gross profit, operating expenses, interest, and depreciation. Make sure you include adjusted earnings to allow prospective buyers to understand the business's discretionary earnings.

Include charts of key ratios if you think it will help buyers. In this summary, you don't want to divulge everything, but you do want to show a buyer how much he can realistically expect to earn based on historical performance.

HINT

INCLUDE ONLY BASIC FINANCIAL INFORMATION IN THE PROFILE. THEN ADD THE FOLLOWING: "DETAILED FINANCIAL INFORMATION AND TAX RETURNS WILL BE MADE AVAILABLE DURING DUE DILIGENCE.

Attachments

At the end of your profile, you can attach any documents that would help the buyer learn more about your business and the industry. Here's a list of examples:

- Brochures
- Product information
- Press clippings
- Industry analysis
- Asset list
- Photographs

Skeletons in the closet

No business is perfect. Nevertheless, you need to handle negative information very carefully so you don't turn good buyers away.

For starters, you have to admit any problems. Don't try to hide weaknesses. If buyers don't see anything on the con side of their pros and cons list, they might be suspicious. Try to position all negative aspects as opportunities for growth or development. If you have recently lost an important customer, for example, show how this creates an opportunity to diversify the customer base.

In many cases, you can explain negatives quite reasonably. Perhaps your retail clothing store suffered a dip in sales for two months while there was construction next door. Or maybe margins became smaller when suppliers raised their prices, which may have affected all companies in your industry equally.

If necessary, blame yourself. Of course, you want to show prospective buyers you ran the business well, but you also want them to believe that they can do a better job. Admitting mistakes and blaming yourself for weaknesses is much better than blaming the business, the industry, or the overall economic climate.

While acknowledging weaknesses, respond to buyers' fears. Reassure them that they can learn to run the business well. Offer to help train them, if possible. But be completely upfront about the abilities a buyer might need to succeed. If a buyer is not cut out to run your business, you'll want to weed him out now. An incapable buyer will bring trouble, especially if you decide to finance the deal yourself.

Things to do

You've seen the major sections of the profile, but there are several things to keep in mind as you work through the profile and before you begin handing out copies:

- **Make it look good**. If you don't have the time or skills, then hire someone to give your profile nice formatting. Print it on quality paper. Make a simple and attractive cover. Present it in a new folder or binder.

- **Make sure it's well written**. If you're not a good writer, have someone else do it. Language is powerful. At the bare minimum, have someone proofread it for errors or weaknesses.

- **Avoid business jargon**. People who buy small businesses don't always have experience in the industry. Your profile has to make sense to someone without knowledge of your type of business.

- **Be completely honest and factual**. If you don't tell the truth, you will probably see deals die in the due diligence phase. If you're not completely honest but still manage to make a deal, you expose yourself to legal liability for misrepresenting your business to the buyer.

- **Create a new email account**. Use this for inquiries by potential buyers. You don't want buyers having any contact with staff through company email or business phone. Remember the importance of confidentiality.

Things not to do

- **Don't make projections on future sales or profits.** Accurate predictions are difficult to make.

- **Don't provide warranties.** You don't want legal troubles if the business doesn't perform exactly as you promise.

- **Don't write the profile like a used car ad or an overpromising sales pitch.** This can turn serious buyers off. Present compelling facts and highlight strengths, but remember that exclamation marks and all-caps won't persuade someone that your business is worth buying.

- **Don't include secrets.** Even with a confidentiality agreement, you need to protect your sensitive information. This might mean trade secrets, client contracts, or customer names.

The Blind Profile

A blind profile is a 1-2 page document that provides a general picture of the business but does not reveal the exact identity of the business or its owner. The profile doesn't give clearly identifiable details such as location, so this document can be given to the public, posted on bulletin boards, mailed, or distributed in any other non-secure way.

The profile should include an overview the following information:

- Type of business
- General location (city, county or state)
- Asking price
- Basic terms
- Year established
- Reason for selling
- Revenues
- Competitive advantages
- Competition
- Growth opportunities

You must write the blind profile in deliberately vague language so that people can't guess exactly which business they are reading about. For example, if you say "large pet store near major amusement park in Wayne County," and you are the only one that fits that description, you're not being vague enough.

Alright, if you've taken the time and energy to create compelling marketing materials, you've also taken a good hard look at your business and can move on to the next stage: Advertising and Finding Buyers.

Module 5: Advertising and Finding Buyers

Introduction

So you've come up with a value for your business, packaged it for sale, recruited a team, and developed your marketing materials. Now it's time to find some buyers. You are looking for potential buyers that not only *want* to run your business but those who *can* run your business.

There are several avenues to pursue when looking for these qualified prospects. The Internet, newspapers, word-of-mouth, and trade publications can all be good sources. This section will cover these sources and others. But the major focus will be on the Internet, because it is by far the number one way in which buyers find businesses.

You'll need to learn how to write an effective advertisement for your business. The exact form your ad takes will depend on where it will appear, but the underlying purpose will always be to get potential buyers interested in moving to the next step while not giving away too much information. You won't have much space for your ad, so learn to focus your writing skills.

Another thing you'll want to do is look at ads for other businesses. Browse the newspaper classifieds. Look at industry publications. And go online where you can see thousands of short ads for different businesses for sale. Which ones jump out at you? Which ones do you pass over without a second thought? Refine your search and find ads for businesses similar to yours. Make a list of things you think you should include. Imagine you're a buyer. What is appealing? What turns you off? Answering these questions will help you draft the best possible ads.

From the beginning of this process, it is critical that you understand the importance of confidentiality. You don't want people to know you're selling your business. That means staff, customers, suppliers, competitors, or any of their friends or neighbors. You need to be in control of the information. You'll read more about how to maintain confidentiality later in this section.

But first, you need to know what your ads should look like.

Writing Your Ads

Write for your audience

Remember, you want to give prospective buyers enough to get them interested and asking for more information. But do you really want everyone calling you? Probably not. You want good, qualified prospective buyers calling you. Nine out of ten people who look at businesses for sale never actually buy a business. You don't want to spend your valuable time talking to that 90%.

Think about your audience. Think about your ideal types of buyers and craft your ads for them. Your ads should eliminate people who are not a good fit, including unqualified or half-interested buyers who are going around kicking tires.

Ads should be short and to-the-point. To do this, you can draw information and ideas straight from your blind profile, but you need to select which pieces very carefully. Remember to describe your business in positive terms, without exaggerating or going over the top. That might mean saying "profitable ladies clothing store" rather than just "ladies clothing store." Don't just tell buyers what it *is*, tell them what it's *like*.

What to include

Consider how people read ad listings. How did *you* read ad listings when you browsed online looking for ads that you thought were effective? People don't read every word. They are looking for keywords, or types of keywords, that will motivate them to stop and read more closely. These keywords will relate to three major topics:

- **Type of Business:** State your general business type, such as hair salon, auto body shop, web design company, music school, or widget manufacturer.

- **Location:** How you describe your location depends on how identifiable you are. The important thing is not to give your identity away. That may mean you need a general location description such as "bustling college town" rather than a specific one like "Manhattan Beach."

- **Price:** Some sellers hesitate to mention this, but remember that many people search by price. If your ad doesn't include a dollar figure, it might be left out of search results.

If an ad doesn't match a potential buyer's expectations on those three points, he or she will definitely stop reading. Beyond these three key points, what can you include?

- **Date of Establishment:** If your business has been around for a while, it's a good idea to mention when it was established. It shows that the business model has been tested through time.

- **3 to 5 Major Strengths:** You took these into consideration when writing a confidential business profile. Examples include excellent lease terms, busy location, training period, loyal customer base, unique products, and increasing profits.

- **Seller Financing:** If you are willing to finance the deal, mention this. List the basic terms of your financing offer, or state that they are negotiable.

- **Your Ideal Buyer:** If your ideal buyer finds a description of himself in your ad, he'll definitely be interested in learning more.

What not to include

You don't want to attract tire kickers, unqualified buyers, poorly matched buyers, or swindlers. You also want to present yourself and your business as honest and strong. For this reason, you should avoid the following:

- **OBO:** Nothing says that you are desperate quite like this common little abbreviation for "or best offer." If you put OBO in your ad, forget about getting close to your asking price.

- **Negative Reasons for Selling:** This could mean divorce, illness, or pending jail time. Some people will think you're desperate to sell, and others will wonder whether the business is on solid ground.

- **Overstatement**: Excessive use of capital letters, italicization, underlining, and exclamation marks will turn serious buyers off. Example: YOU CAN'T AFFORD TO PASS THIS UP!!!!! Also watch your wording. You need to describe your business positively, but saying things like "absolutely phenomenal business opportunity" is too much.

- **Identifying Information**: Just like the blind profile, your ads should not reveal the identity or exact location of your business.

How to Maintain Confidentiality

Confidentiality is important even if some people already know you're trying to sell your business. You may decide to share your intentions of selling with key employees or other people. Be sure they understand not to tell anyone about the sale without getting your approval first. Confidentiality covers more than just the *fact* that you are selling. It also covers sensitive information in your marketing materials.

To repeat, there are two aspects of confidentiality: 1) the fact that you're selling, and 2) sensitive information related to your business operations.

For example, your confidential business profile contains financial information and other things that you might not want to get into the wrong hands. Further on in the process, you might also be revealing tax returns, contract details, pending patents, and similar matters to a potential buyer.

So, how do you maintain confidentiality?

Non-Disclosure Agreement /Confidentiality Agreement: If a buyer has not signed a legal document promising secrecy, you will have no recourse or control over the dissemination of your sensitive information.

Don't Use Your Regular Contact Numbers and Addresses: Email addresses, phone numbers, and street addresses can identify you or your business. You don't want that. You can easily create a new email address that you use to field inquiries from buyers. Even if you regularly use a non-identifying email address, having a separate one can help organize your work. For telephone inquiries, you can get a prepaid cell phone or have a friend or associate field inquiries. For fax inquiries, you can use an online provider of virtual fax numbers like eFax. For a mailing address, you can use a friend, your accountant , or your attorney. If you are a good client, a professional shouldn't charge you for this. You can also get a post office box.

If you set up clear procedures for confidentiality and stick to them, you shouldn't have to worry about whether the wrong people are learning the wrong things.

Where to Post Ads

Fish where the fish are. Consider who is likely to buy your business and advertise in the places they are likely to see.

The Internet

Remember that the Internet remains your single best resource. It has been estimated that 90% of all initial buyer inquiries for businesses under $1 million come through Internet listings.

There are many websites dedicated solely to helping people sell their small businesses. Many of these are quite pricey, charging more than $50 per month for a very basic listing without any photos. But considering the amount of money at stake and the fact that most buyers are browsing online listings, it may be worth it. Just make sure you pick the right one.

You can also try free sites such as Craigslist, industry-hosted websites, and online classifieds of local newspapers. Cast a wide net. Advertise in as many places as possible. You may have to tweak your ad for different requirements, but the basics will remain the same.

Photos are great if you can include them without identifying your business. Listings with photographs always receive more views than those without, no matter what is being sold.

Print media

There are still people who read newspapers, and if those people fit your buyer profile, by all means advertise in the newspaper. Go beyond your local newspaper. Many buyers are looking to relocate themselves or their families, and if you know where they might be coming from, then advertise in those places as well.

Many industries publish magazines and newsletters which may have a section for businesses for sale. There may also be small publications for entrepreneurs or small business owners that could yield buyer inquiries. Don't consider any avenue too small or insignificant. It's little extra effort, and you might just find the right buyer this way.

Direct advertising

You don't necessarily have to wait for people to find your ad. Consider going straight to them. You'll need names and addresses, and you may be able to get your hands on industry lists or lists of similar companies. Your attorney, accountant, or bookkeeper may be sitting on hundreds of good leads. And you can ask one of these professionals to include your blind profile in his or her newsletter or to send letters on your behalf.

Business brokers

Business brokerages are an obvious place to go when you want to get the word out. They take careful inventory of buyers and the types of businesses they're looking for. They have access to a huge network of people. The decision to use a broker, however, involves more than just paying for a listing. If you have trouble finding enough qualified buyers for your business, you may want to consider listing with a broker.

> **WARNING**
>
> SOME SHADY BUSINESS BROKERS WILL TELL YOU THAT THEY HAVE BUYERS FOR YOUR BUSINESS JUST TO GET YOU TO SIGN AN EXCLUSIVE LISTING AGREEMENT.
>
> THE TRUTH IS, IF YOU OFFER A REASONABLE PRICE AND FAIR TERMS, INTERESTED BUYERS FROM YOUR AREA WILL FIND YOUR ONLINE AND/OR NEWSPAPER ADS.

Finishing Up

After you have written your ads, put confidentiality procedures in place, and posted ads where you think buyers will see them, you're ready for the next step: Responding to and Screening Buyers. Take a deep breath. The real fun is about to begin.

Module 6:
Responding to and Screening Buyers

Introduction

You've placed your ads, sent out some emails, and hired team members to put the word out. Now you wait for the phone to ring and the inbox to start filling up.

Depending on how broadly you've advertised and the attractiveness of your price and terms, you may start getting quite a few inquiries. Right from the start, you have to be prepared with a strategy and stick to your process.

An overwhelming majority of people who inquire about businesses for sale never actually buy one. You want to limit the time you spend communicating with those people. You may also be surprised by the number of people who simply request that you send over all financial information so they can consider things and get back to you if they're interested. Again, stick to your process. These people are being unreasonable.

Right from the beginning, think about how you want to manage inquiries. You should have already decided on this when you posted your ads. In most cases, sellers ask for emails or phone messages. You may get a few, or you may get lots. Regardless, you want to handle things calmly and carefully. Don't get too excited. Understand that not everyone who calls is a ready and capable buyer.

In fact, there are several types of people that you may encounter.

Types of Prospects

Some people don't fit neatly into stereotypes, but most prospective buyers will fall into a few broad categories.

Wishful-thinkers: The name says it all. They can take up a lot of your time with their questions, but they may not be qualified or capable. And they may get along quite far in the process before bailing out at the last minute. Many day-dreamers will not have thought through the financing side of things and will not ask you the questions that you think a potential buyer should be asking. In fact, they may not ask many questions at all.

Tire-kickers: These people may or may not be serious about buying a business. Regardless, they haven't yet, and they probably won't any time soon. This is why you ask people how long they've been looking. Anyone who says "two years" is probably this type. They can take up a whole lot of your time with what *seem* like relevant questions. Tire-kickers can be tough to identify right off the bat, and some tire-kickers do eventually get behind the wheel, but beware.

Snoops: There are people out there who are simply looking for information. The most likely snoop is a competitor, but it could be anyone else who wants to know how your business or your type of business operates. Again, stick to your process. You might be able to expose Snoops quite easily, or they may simply back off once they realize information sharing is a two-way street.

Wolves: Wolves sniff around for desperate sellers. They hope to snag a good deal and somehow turn a profit a little further down the road. A wolf may show undue interest in your reasons for selling, or he might focus on the negative aspects of your business. This type of buyer is not necessarily someone to avoid. Maybe you *are* desperate and need a quick sale. In certain circumstances, you might be willing to settle for much less than your asking price, and a wolf might be a welcome figure.

Qualified buyers: These are the people who deserve your attention. They understand what they're getting into, they have the financial means, and they're serious about running a business. Some of them have a specific type of business in mind, but others are quite open to different opportunities. Those that are open might require more work on your end. But if they know that yours is the type of business they want, then your job is that much easier.

Keeping Track of Prospects

You need to keep careful track of the people who contact you and details of your interactions. Don't rely on memory. Make a system. It could be as sophisticated as a database or as simple as a notebook with a new page for each prospective buyer. Start documenting your interactions immediately. You might get excited about the first few people who call you, but if the phone starts ringing all day, you are probably not going to remember everything you need to.

What do you need to document? The more, the better. At minimum, you should have phone numbers, email addresses, line of work, and a record of what information you have exchanged with each person. If someone calls back a couple of weeks after first inquiring, you need to know exactly what level you got to with that person. Has he signed a confidentiality agreement? Have you sent him your Confidential Business Profile? If you don't know these things, you won't know what you can and can't say in the conversation.

You can also take notes on people's backgrounds, their family members, warning signs, apparent financial means, how they found out about your business, and anything else that might prove useful in the future.

Don't forget: when you are contacted by a new prospect, have the person sign a confidentiality agreement as soon as possible.

The Confidentiality Agreement

You may hear this referred to as a non-disclosure agreement. Same idea: people who sign this agreement are promising they will not share with anybody the information that you give to them.

HINT

YOU CAN PURCHASE A GENERIC CA OR NDA AT LEGALZOOM.COM OR YOUR ATTORNEY CAN DRAFT THIS DOCUMENT FOR YOU.

Anything you say to an individual who has *not* signed a confidentiality agreement becomes public knowledge. Limit what you say before this agreement is in place. Only one person will end up buying your business, but all those other people you dealt with will also have the information.

A legitimate buyer will understand this fact and have no hesitation about signing the agreement. If a wise prospect knows you've been sharing information too freely, it increases the risk of that person's investment. So strictly enforcing confidentiality protects your eventual buyer, not just you.

In all of your interactions with buyers, they will ask you to reveal information. People will call and ask you questions. Even after the confidentiality agreement is in place, you will encounter questions you may not be comfortable answering. That's OK. Tell the buyer that you'll get back to him on that question to buy yourself some time. In these circumstances, you need to strike a balance between your confidentiality and the prospect's legitimate need for information. If you can't (or don't want to) answer a question, tell the person you can't. If you can figure out the reason behind his or her request, then try to find a way of addressing the concern without giving details.

For example, if a prospect is worried that you might be too reliant on a few big customers, he might ask for a customer list. You don't want to give him that. But you know what he's worried about, so you can give him a chart that outlines revenue by unnamed customer.

Talking With Prospective Buyers

In your initial dealings with prospective buyers, you need to be prepared to deflect difficult or unreasonable questions. You will also have a lot of questions that *you* want to ask, so there will be a lot of information being exchanged. What you want is to control the conversation and the flow of information.

To do this, give the buyer an overview of the process. The process will probably look something like this:

- Prospective buyer signs confidentiality agreement
- Seller sends confidential business profile
- Prospective buyer sends a list of questions
- Seller sends answers to questions
- Arrange a face-to-face meeting
- Arrange a site visit
- Letter of Intent or Contingent offer
- Due diligence
- Closing

Tell people this is how it works, and stick to your process.

Of course, in an initial telephone conversation a prospect may want to dig for a bit of information. Or a lot of information. You may want to dig for some information as well to find out if the prospect is worth your time. Just don't let the other person control the conversation. If you feel comfortable answering these questions now, go for it. Do so simply and then ask a question of your own. Proceed slowly and thoughtfully. Don't get led into revealing sensitive information.

Here are some of the first questions a prospective buyer may want to ask:

- What are your reasons for selling?
- How did you arrive at your asking price?

- Will you offer financing?
- How long has the business been in operation?
- How long have you owned the business?
- Will you stay on for a training period?
- How much can a new owner expect in monthly earnings?
- What's so special about your business?

Here are some of the first questions that you may want to ask of a prospective buyer:

- How did you find out about this opportunity?
- What is your experience in owning or working for a small business?
- Why are you interested in buying a business?
- How long have you been looking to buy a business?
- What is your timeframe for buying a business?
- What do you currently do?
- Is your buying decision being made with someone else, like a partner or spouse?
- How much cash do you have on hand that you'd be willing to invest in a business?
- Are you comfortable with a credit check?

Buyer Reactions

Some people are going to be angry that you simply won't send them your five-year financials after the initial phone call. This disrespect for your process is a warning sign. You can bet that if they're difficult to deal with in the beginning, they'll be difficult to deal with the entire way.

Some people will react very negatively to your request for a confidentiality agreement or financial information. Don't take this personally. Serious buyers with an understanding of business will not hesitate because they know that it is standard procedure and protects the person who eventually buys the business.

Some people will seem to vanish after the initial inquiry or further along in the process. Don't mistake this as a lack of interest. People are busy. They may like your business but be looking at a huge number of other potential opportunities and talking to plenty of other sellers and brokers. If they appear to have potential, follow up. Remind them about *your* opportunity.

NOTE

REMIND BUYERS THAT YOUR BUSINESS IS FOR SALE BY OWNER. BUYERS TYPICALLY LIKE THIS BECAUSE THEY BELIEVE THEY ARE ALMOST ALWAYS GUARANTEED A BETTER DEAL.

Some people will appear extremely interested and want to accelerate the process. Proceed with caution. It may be someone who is genuinely interested and capable, but it may not. Again: stick to your process. Don't get so excited about the fact that someone wants to buy your business that you overlook the fact that you need to find the *right* person to buy your business.

Next Steps

After the initial conversation, and after a prospect has signed a confidentiality agreement, you're ready to start revealing some information. At this point, you can send your Confidential Business Profile, preferably by email. After the buyer reviews your Profile, he can submit a list of questions to you. You can take your time crafting good responses to those questions and pose some of your own.

There are good reasons to conduct your dealings with potential buyers in writing. You can take the time to provide good responses and avoid revealing confidential information in the excited flow of conversation. A written record also serves as a reference point for future discussions and negotiations. Writing can save time because you can keep a file of stock answers for common questions which you can then copy and paste into an email. Email correspondence can help you screen buyers. Have a close look at the prospect's messages. If they are poorly or hastily written, unclear or vague, or too brief or unprofessional, then you may want to file the prospect in the cold pile. Inexperienced people may also complain about the process or think that corresponding by email is inconvenient. Be careful of such people. Once again: stick to your process.

After the exchange of questions, it is time for a face-to-face meeting in a neutral location such as an attorney or accountant's office, a coffee shop, or a restaurant. If this meeting goes well, and you think that the buyer is ready and capable, you can arrange a tour of your facility.

After each discussion or exchange with a potential buyer, wait a couple of days and then follow up. Ask for feedback and concerns. Make sure you record the outcome of each interaction and any reasons a buyer might have for backing out of the opportunity.

Initial Screening

Remember that you're looking for the *right* buyer for your business, not just any buyer. This is especially important if you are going to be financing the deal. You will continue to have a vested interest in the business for a number of years and must have complete confidence in the new owner's ability to generate profits.

Throughout your discussions and exchanges, you need to be asking yourself questions about the prospect. Here are some of the important ones:

- Is the buyer prepared?
- Does the buyer respect your time and confidentiality?
- Does the buyer provide explanation or justification for his ideas, like objection to your asking price?
- Does the buyer know what he is talking about?
- Does the buyer *pretend* to know what he is talking about?
- Can you see yourself going the distance with this person as a *partner*?

That last question is very important. If you know for certain a potential buyer does *not* meet your expectations, there is no reason to carry him any further. You do not owe anyone a facility tour or more information simply out of courtesy.

Rank your prospects. Give priority to the best ones. Spend your time wisely.

> **HINT**
>
> **BE OPEN TO GOOD PROSPECTS THAT DO NOT NECESSARILY FIT THE IMAGE OF THE IDEAL BUYER THAT YOU'VE CREATED IN YOUR MIND. TOO MANY SELLERS WILL DISQUALIFY BUYERS FOR THE WRONG REASONS AND MISS EXCELLENT OPPORTUNITIES IN THE PROCESS.**
>
> **FOR EXAMPLE, DON'T ASSUME THAT A HEAVY FOREIGN ACCENT INDICATES LACK OF ABILITY. PAY ALL POTENTIAL BUYERS EQUAL RESPECT AND ATTENTION AND EVALUATE THEM ACCORDING TO UNBIASED CRITERIA.**

The Business Tour

For those special prospective buyers, a site visit can produce a lot of excitement. The idea of owning a business suddenly becomes much more real. If you're prepared, it's an excellent chance to show off your facility and demonstrate why your business is the best choice among all the others that a buyer may be looking at.

The important thing to remember is that bit about "special prospective buyers." Only truly capable, interested, and qualified prospective buyers should make it far enough in your screening process to reach the point of touring your business facility. A buyer should never move to this step without having seen the Confidential Business Profile.

There are reasons not to open up this stage to too many prospects. Arranging a site visit and doing one well are not easy. It may be very time-consuming to prepare properly, it may be very difficult to schedule, and it has the potential to unnerve employees. What follows are the basics of making a business tour impressive and worthwhile for those truly good prospects.

Preparation

The very first module ("Getting Ready to Sell") suggested cleaning up the physical aspects of your business location. If you haven't done such things by this time, do them now. Here are a few suggestions:

- Dispose of unused equipment and machines
- Give everything a thorough cleaning
- Replace broken light bulbs and fixtures
- Tidy up the entrance way
- Wash the windows
- Organize workspaces

It's not unusual for business owners to get a bit lazy in terms of organization and cleanliness. You may have become accustomed to a certain amount of dirt and disarray, but now you should be looking at your business through the eyes of a prospect. Imagine *you* are touring the facility for the first time. Then plan your preparation accordingly and make your premises as attractive as possible.

Besides making things neat and organized, you should plan exactly what you are going to show the prospect and have at least a rough outline of what you will say. Part of your tour may include a special display or demonstration. Show off the great parts of your facility and any products or processes that hold special appeal. All of this preparation should be customized to suit the specific background, interest, or desires of a prospect. By now, you should have learned something about the prospective buyer.

You will also want to make sure you have a comfortable place to sit down for a meeting after the tour is finished. If your facility simply can't accommodate such a meeting, choose a suitable place nearby. One final thing you need to consider is whether the tour will take place during business hours. If so, you must decide what you will say to employees or customers. If needed, you can introduce the prospect as a business associate or friend, without going into too much detail about the purpose.

Scheduling a tour

If possible or suitable, you should try to arrange a tour after-hours or on the weekend. You want to minimize interruptions and have ample time and privacy for any explanations.

For many businesses, such as restaurants and retail stores, it may be best to witness the action during normal business hours. Even if you don't believe it's necessary, some buyers will insist on it. If this is the case, then make sure you conduct the tour very carefully. You'll need to explain your concerns about confidentiality and brief the prospect on what you've told the employees about the visit.

Either way, you want to make sure you have plenty of time after the tour for discussion. There may be things you need to explain, questions you or the buyer wants to ask, and even key points to negotiate. Neither you nor the buyer should have to rush off to an appointment right after the tour.

The Tour

Ideally, you should sit down with the buyer before the tour for a brief discussion. If this is the first time you've met the person, try to build a positive rapport. Small talk at the beginning of a sales process or negotiation can have a very positive effect on the outcome. Ask about the buyer's current work, family, aspirations, or background. Reveal something about yourself during this initial encounter as well. Be friendly. People like to buy from people they like. Moreover, this small talk will help you understand a bit more about the buyer, which will help you customize the tour.

In your initial discussion, you can preview the tour for the prospect. Explain what the buyer is going to see. Remind him of the confidentiality issue. Ask if there's anything in particular the buyer is curious about.

> **NOTE**
>
> ALTHOUGH THE FINANCIAL ASPECTS OF A BUSINESS ARE IMPORTANT, BUYING A BUSINESS MAY BE A HIGHLY EMOTIONAL DECISION. IT COULD BE THE FULFILLMENT OF A LIFELONG DREAM OR THE TICKET TO FREEDOM FROM BOSSES. DON'T FORGET THIS AS YOU SHOW A PROSPECT AROUND!

During the actual tour, maintain focus on the physical aspects of the business. Explain products, processes, and people. Save discussion of financial matters for later. Highlight strengths, but don't avoid the negatives. Answer questions openly and honestly. If the tour takes place while employees are working, avoid discussion or questions that might threaten to reveal the purpose of the visit. You can debrief and answer concerns later.

After the tour you should sit down for a meeting in a private space. During this meeting the buyer will probably have many questions about what they have seen. You may also have things you want to explain in greater detail that you couldn't during the tour itself.

Continue to screen the buyer. This meeting is a perfect time to ask questions that you haven't yet had a chance to, such as:

- What is your past business experience?
- What is your timeline for purchasing a business?
- How long have you been looking?

- How will you finance the purchase?
- Do you have cash reserves to support your lifestyle during the transition period?
- Who else is involved in the decision?

Of course, you've only given the best and most qualified prospects a site tour, but an in-person discussion can usually reveal a lot more about a person than an email exchange or phone call.

This post-tour meeting might be the right time to start negotiating. A ready and eager buyer could start discussing price and terms. Don't shy away from such a discussion, but steer things toward getting a Letter of Intent from the buyer. Even if the buyer is not itching to negotiate, you may want to talk about several important aspects of your selling process. Tell the person your rough timeline for accepting Letters of Intent, how much time you would like to see for due diligence, and a closing date target.

Keep in mind: the prospect has just received a lot of information and seen a lot of new things. He or she will most likely want to take some time to reflect and will probably think of several important questions later the same day. You may also think of several points you wished you had mentioned. For this reason, tell the buyer that you will follow up in two to three days to answer any further questions and, if everything looks great, move on to the next step, which is a Letter of Intent.

Letter of Intent

A Letter of Intent is a document that states the major elements of a potential sale, as agreed upon by you and the prospective buyer. You may receive Letters of Intent from one or several prospects, but you will only choose one. When you accept a Letter of Intent, you may be agreeing to deal exclusively with that buyer.

A typical Letter of Intent includes:

- Selling price and terms (down payment, financing term, interest rate, etc.)
- How the sale price is broken down (tangible assets, goodwill, etc.)
- Timelines (due diligence phase, closing date deadline, etc.)
- Contingencies (accounting review, lease transfer, etc.)

It's perfectly normal to negotiate these Letters of Intent. But do so carefully, because it's virtually impossible to improve a deal from your standpoint *after* the Letter of Intent. The price may be negotiated downward through the due diligence phase and you should try to address all price issues now. This will be the best deal you can get.

It is in your best interest to have more than one Letter of Intent for consideration. You are not obligated to accept any one of them until the terms are reasonable. If you do have several Letters to consider, do so very carefully.

The sale price is only one of the things you're looking at. Think about the terms of the sale. Think about the buyer's capabilities, especially if you're financing the deal. What's better, an inexperienced buyer offering $200,000 or an experienced buyer offering $175,000? With the former, you might never see your money or wind up with the business again after the buyer has run it into the ground.

Another thing to pay close attention to is the due diligence period. A two-month period is too long because other prospects will lose interest. That means you're left in a weak bargaining position. 2 – 3 weeks for due diligence should be enough for most small businesses.

Congratulations! If you've made it this far, you probably feel very close to getting a deal done. You *should* feel excited, but remember there are still a couple of very tough steps before you actually close a deal and hand over the keys to the new owner of your business.

Module 7:
Negotiating a Deal

Introduction

Negotiating a deal means coming to agreement with the buyer on all the aspects of the business sale. Throughout this process, you and the buyer should remember and remind each other that you both ultimately want to get a mutually satisfactory deal done in a timely fashion. It's easy to get stuck in all the details, and inexperienced buyers and sellers may feel that giving up anything means they're getting a bum deal. That's not how it works. You never get everything you want.

And don't expect this to be fast. Negotiating the terms of the deal can take anywhere from a few days to a few weeks. Avoid lengthy delays that kill momentum, but don't push for a deal to come together overnight. Keep the conversation going, and pay attention to what matters most. A good deal offers you the right protection, especially if you're financing the deal. Failure to protect yourself might mean you never see your money.

Call on your team. You'll need your accountant to help you sort out the tax implications of different sale structures and terms, and you'll need a lawyer to help you draft the final sales contract. You and the buyer may decide to hire a neutral attorney to draft the closing documents. You can share this attorney's fee and then have your own lawyers review and comment on the document. This not only helps you save money but also prevents the buyer's lawyer from trying to stack the contract in his client's favor.

This book presents an overview of negotiation and sale structures, but you will need legal help with the sale of your particular business. Doing this on your own has limits, and this book cannot replace an attorney, accountant or professional advisor.

At negotiation time, you're going to be considering four major points:

- Price
- Payment terms
- Assets
- Price allocation

Before learning more about these four points, you need to understand the two basic types of sale.

Types of Sale

The two basic types of sale are referred to as an "Asset Sale" and a "Stock Sale."

In an asset sale, you are selling some or all of your company's assets. Debts, liabilities, and legal claims are not included in this sale, and for this reason most buyers prefer this type. Asset sales are by far the most common type of sale, and if you're a sole proprietorship or a partnership, this is the only type that applies to you. As the seller, you may choose to remove certain assets from the sale. Many people do not include cash and accounts receivable, for example. At the same time, you will have to resolve all debts and liabilities at closing.

In a stock sale, you are selling a corporation or LLC along with the assets owned by the entity. This form of transaction rarely occurs in small business deals. If your business is not organized as a corporation or LLC, then this isn't even an option. A stock sale may or may not include liabilities, debts, and legal claims. While an entity sale normally includes more than an asset sale does, the seller and buyer can still negotiate certain assets or liabilities out of the sale.

If you are organized as a corporation or LLC, you will have to carefully choose the type of sale to pursue. The tax implications of each type are very different, and professional advice can help you understand what is best in your situation.

Price

The first and most obvious point you may be negotiating is price. At this stage of the game, you may have already dealt with much of the negotiation around price. The letter of intent includes a price, and that figure serves as your *starting point*. Negotiation and due diligence might move this number, and this movement will almost always be in one direction: downward.

Why might the price move downward?

The buyer may suggest a price reduction because of what he discovers through due diligence. For example, the condition of equipment might not be satisfactory or the future potential of the business you outlined appears too optimistic. The buyer may have also overestimated the amount of money that he has to put toward the purchase price and underestimate the amount he needs in transition.

Buyers may also ask for price reductions in exchange for price allocation or terms that favor you. If you want a large down payment, for example, the buyer might only agree if the final purchase price is lower.

This involves negotiation, which means you should try to get something whenever you give something. If the buyer requests or demands a lower price, ask for something in return. Whether it's better terms, a faster payment period, or better allocation, you have to feel it's a fair trade.

Payment Terms

As you learned in module 3, all-cash deals for small businesses are extremely rare, partly because anyone with enough cash to buy a small business is probably not interested in *running* a small business. And banks are very reluctant to lend money to small business buyers, or accept the business as security, especially if the value of tangible assets does not make up most of the purchase price. So where does the money come from?

Here are the benefits of seller financing, as outlined in Module 3:

- It shows faith in the potential of the business
- It discourages price reductions
- It helps close the deal faster
- It allows more flexibility in terms
- It stretches earnings over several years, which reduces the seller's taxes
- It generates interest income

Most sellers will get a certain amount of the purchase price as a down payment and defer payment on the remainder. The pieces of this equation that will be subject to negotiation are:

- The size of the down payment
- The financing period
- The interest rate
- The nature of the deferred payment

Your first thought might be that you want to get as much of the purchase price as possible on closing day. While this may be generally true, seller financing means you retain a vested interest in the business. So a down payment that leaves the buyer without the means to support himself in transition does not work in your favor. Your tax advisor may also tell you that stretching the earnings out over several years can prevent a large tax bill for the year of the sale.

The deferred payment may take a few different forms. It may be a regular payment schedule just like you'd arrange on a bank loan. It may also include a large balloon payment after a certain period, which allows the buyer a chance to have lower monthly payments at first and allows you to receive full payment sooner. It could also include earn-out payments that are partly dependent on the continued success of the business.

Assets

You must decide exactly what is included in the sale. It doesn't matter whether it is a so-called "asset sale" or "entity sale." You still need to have a list of included assets.

Remember the two types of assets:

- **Tangible assets** (furniture, fixtures, equipment, inventory, real estate)
- **Intangible assets** (copyrights, patents, accounts receivable, supplier contracts, goodwill)

At the beginning of the sale process, you listed all of these items and their estimated or exact worth. That original list may not be what is included in the end. The buyer might not want certain assets and remove them from the sale with a corresponding price adjustment. On the flipside, you may respond to requests for price reduction by removing assets from the sale. This makes sense if you can turn around and sell those assets individually.

Asset Allocation

In an asset sale, not all assets are taxed equally. The government will view some as capital gains but others as regular income. For this reason, how you break the price down among the different assets can affect how much tax both buyer and seller pay. The buyer and seller can't allocate the price differently. There is a single IRS Form 8594 that lays out the sale structure.

An allocation that reduces taxes for the seller will usually increase taxes for the buyer, and vice versa. This can be a sticking point in the negotiation.

For example, the amount you earn on goodwill is taxed as a capital gain, which comes with a lower rate than regular income. However, the buyer is required to amortize his purchase of goodwill over a period of 15 years, which makes it more difficult for him to lower his future taxes. So you will be arguing for a greater goodwill allocation while the buyer will be arguing for a lower goodwill allocation.

Now consider inventory. This is taxed as regular income for the seller, but the buyer can write it off as an expense as soon as he buys it. So you will be arguing for a lower inventory allocation while the buyer will be arguing for a greater inventory allocation.

This might seem to add another frustrating layer of complexity to the entire process, but it may actually increase your negotiating power. In exchange for a price reduction, you can get an allocation that saves you more in taxes than you are losing on the reduction. A tax advisor or accountant can help you figure out how this might work.

Other Aspects of the Sale

Besides price, terms, assets, and allocation, the sales contract may include a few other agreements, all of which may come into the negotiation.

- **Non-compete agreement:** the buyer will want you to guarantee that you won't set up shop across the street in direct competition with your former business. The agreement usually stipulates certain types of business within a certain region for a certain period. In order to be legally binding, the buyer must pay you for this agreement, so it must be part of the price allocation.

- **Employment contract:** there may be knowledge, relationships, and processes that take time to transfer to a new owner, and the buyer might want to employ you for a certain period to help with this transfer. Make sure that the exact terms of this agreement, including period, duties, and compensation, are clearly laid out.

- **Consulting agreement:** instead of employment, you might agree to a basic consulting agreement. Again, the period and compensation should be laid out clearly.

Some Points about Negotiation

First and foremost, you should remember that it's in the interest of both parties to get a deal done in a timely manner. This requires give and take on both sides.

Second, remember that there is no substitute for good preparation. Discuss all the different possibilities with your accountant and lawyer before and during the negotiation process. In the beginning, figure out what your bottom line is and what your deal-breakers are. Then follow your plan. Learn as much as you can about the buyer so that you can respond to his concerns and arguments.

If you're prepared and have your sights set on the right deal, you'll do well. Some other things to keep in mind:

- **Maintain momentum:** respond quickly to buyer concerns, keep in constant contact, and don't allow for long delays.
- **Negotiate with the right people:** if you learned early on that the seller will be making his decision with someone else, such as a

spouse or a business partner, then make sure you're negotiating with all of those people in the room.

- **Protect yourself:** maintain confidentiality and take care of all the legal details.

- **Keep an open mind:** if you expect the buyer to accept everything you want, you won't get a deal done. Be receptive to creative solutions to obstacles.

- **Don't argue for a price increase:** it simply won't happen!

- **Look for win-win solutions:** both people need to be satisfied with the deal.

Module 8:
Due Diligence

Introduction

An offer or letter of intent from a qualified and capable buyer does not mean you've got a done deal. That offer is conditional on a complete inspection of your business and the claims you have made about it. This is called due diligence.

Plan to spend some time in the due diligence phase. It is normal and necessary, although it may seem a little frightening because you are opening everything up for close inspection.

Don't worry too much, because the only people to make it to this stage are those who truly qualify and have maintained confidentiality through the earlier stages.

Buyers will be looking for things that are not quite as positive as you made them out to be. They'll be keeping an eye out for problems which they will then use in negotiation. Minor issues will reduce the price, but major issues might sink the entire deal.

If you are organized, prepared and haven't attempted to hide negative information during your dealings with the buyer, then due diligence won't be painful. It is true that half of all business deals die during this phase, but that usually happens because a) the buyer is not truly qualified, or b) the seller has not been completely upfront.

Your Preparation

Preparing for due diligence involves collecting and organizing all the paperwork that a buyer will want to see. Don't wait until the buyer requests these documents. Having them ready will inspire confidence in your business and move the process along more quickly.

Just like in negotiation, momentum is important. If the buyer has to wait a few days for you to gather certain papers, a good deal may stall. This process can be frightening for buyers as well. They've invested a lot of time and energy and obviously see your business as a good opportunity. They will be worried about what may come out in due diligence. If you are pleasant and cooperative, you will relieve the buyer's fears. On the other hand, if you drag your feet or make the buyer feel you're being uncooperative, he may feel suspicious.

You may have already prepared many of the documents required in due diligence. That's great, but some things, such as inventory, might have changed since you first presented them. Other things may need to be reorganized; for example, the buyer may only have seen your *recast* financials.

Things to Keep in Mind

A deal feels close, but don't break out the champagne. During due diligence, your business still needs you.

- **Confidentiality:** Remind buyers of the ongoing importance of confidentiality. Maintain contact through private channels, such as non-work email or phone, or through your accountant or lawyer. The deal may still fall through, in which case someone will walk away with a lot of very sensitive information. Just to be safe, you can ask buyers to inspect information on your premises or in the office of one of your team's professionals. If you really need to release documents to the buyer, make a record of it so that you can make sure they're returned.

- **Business as Usual:** Don't get lazy about running your business during due diligence. It might limit your bargaining power. Your laziness can also affect employee performance, and that can threaten a potential deal. Due diligence will require a lot of your time, but keep your business running in tip-top shape during this period.

- **Manage Access to Customers:** The buyer might want to find out more about your customers. He might even want to talk to them directly. Avoid this, if possible, by answering questions about customers yourself. If this is not enough, then you'll have to allow the buyer access. But make sure you supervise and facilitate this process.

- **Manage Access to Employees:** It is difficult to completely avoid buyer contact with employees, but you can manage this contact. For starters, try to make this one of the last steps, just in case things fall apart. Second, you can limit contact to key personnel. Let these people know about the situation and have them sign a confidentiality agreement. There is no guarantee that your employees will be agreeable to the potential sale, and you may want to offer incentives for them to stay on with a new owner. The buyer might also want to offer incentives. Third, arrange for meetings between the buyer and employees away from your business premises so that other employees and customers don't become suspicious.

Elements of Due Diligence

What follows is a list of the aspects of your business that a buyer will want to investigate. There might be other items that are important within your industry or your particular business.

- **Tax Returns:** You'll need the at least the past three years and possibly the past five.

- **Detailed Financial Statements:** You'll need three to five years. Make sure they're organized and professional-looking. Remember that the buyer might only have seen your recast financials.

- **Lease:** A buyer will want to see all the terms of the lease, not just rate and term. He will also want to confirm transferability.

- **Contracts:** This includes supplier agreements, franchise agreements, customer/client agreements, employee contracts, and any other B2B or individual legal agreements. Buyers will check closely for transferability.

- **Licenses and Permits:** Buyers will pay close attention to the conditions for renewal of licenses and permits.

- **Intellectual Property Documentation:** This includes certificates or official documentation of patents, copyrights, trademarks, processes, procedures and service marks.

- **Operations:** Information about your operations includes everything from production processes to billing.

- **Real Estate:** This includes mortgages, deeds of trust, surveys, and any liens or debts that may affect title to a property.

- **Equipment/Furnishings List:** A buyer will want to see titles to major pieces of equipment as well as agreements for any leased equipment.

- **Employee Records:** This is to verify labor costs and employment history. Consult your attorney before problems or disputes with employees.

- **Accounts Receivable:** Accounts receivable are not included in most small business sales, but if they are, the buyer will want to see the status of such accounts as well as the payment history of regular accounts.

- **Inventory:** Some buyers will want to count every single item while others will be satisfied with a brief inspection.

Accounts receivable and inventory can be very sticky aspects of due diligence. Their values have already directly affected your initial asking price, but the values have probably changed since you determined that price.

This will affect the final sales price of the business, but don't let it kill the deal. With a little bit of planning and preparation, you should have good explanations for any changes.

The important thing is that you don't let things slide. Some business sellers become lazy about collecting outstanding accounts. Others cut corners on inventory and end up with too much old and discontinued inventory or more raw materials than finished goods.

Warning Signs

Remember, the buyer is looking for problems. Here is a list of possible deal-breakers. If you notice anything here that applies to you, fix it fast or at least be upfront about it:

- **Tax Problems:** If you are being audited or the taxes are not up-to-date, buyers will flee.
- **Environmental Issues:** This could mean you have violated environmental standards or that you are liable for an environmental problem such as a chemical spill or improper disposal of waste.
- **Unrecorded Liabilities:** Small debts can become major obstacles, even if they were the result of an honest mistake. Unrecorded liabilities often relate to money or time owed to employees.
- **Deferred Maintenance:** Buyers will want to confirm the age and quality of your equipment and vehicles. Some sellers create problems in this area when they don't do regular maintenance because they're going to sell.
- **Litigation:** Any past or pending lawsuit may spell trouble, especially if it relates to product or service liability.

Your Due Diligence on the Buyer

Due diligence goes both ways. Your due diligence on buyers started as soon as you began asking them questions. Anyone who has made it to the point of conducting due diligence on your business has already shown that he is qualified and capable. Now it's time for you to ensure the buyer has not misrepresented himself.

There are five basic things you are going to look at:

- **Financial Statements:** A buyer who is financially capable shouldn't hesitate to prove it. You have revealed sensitive information about your business, so it's only fair that a buyer do the same in return.

- **Credit History:** You might want to save the credit check for the end because it will cost you money and can actually reduce a person's credit score. When you are ready, you'll need the buyer's full name, social security number, and current address. Any of the three big credit-reporting agencies is fine.

- **Resume:** Qualifying a buyer is not much different from interviewing a potential manager. Examine a person's background, experience, and skills to evaluate his ability to run your business.

- **Other Opinions:** Besides checking the buyer's resume references, talk to anyone else you know who has had dealings with the individual. Go to licensing agencies and local courts to find out if the buyer has had any licensing issues or been involved in lawsuits. And don't forget that a simple Google search can turn up a lot of useful information about a person.

- **Business Plan:** The buyer may not have a fully developed and bound business plan for a business he has not yet purchased, but he must have some idea of his plans. If he can put something in writing, that's great. If not, you can at least sit down with him and talk about it.

- **Momentum:** The due diligence phase needs time and close attention, but don't let your momentum with a buyer die. Balance your concerns. You can't afford to enter into a deal with the wrong person, but it's a shame to lose a deal with the right person.

Module 9:
Closing and
Transition

Introduction

You're almost there. If you've worked successfully through due diligence, then you're entering the closing and transition phase. Get excited, but don't head off on vacation yet. Closing the deal and transitioning successfully out of your role as owner can be complicated and frustrating. It's much more than just shaking hands and giving up the keys. There are decisions to be made, activities to coordinate, documents to sign, and people to inform of the change. Every business sale and transition is different, so there is no easy formula for success.

Having a good attorney at this stage of the game is key. Unless your deal is very small and simple, you'll need the help of a seasoned pro. Failing to protect yourself and to consider all the legal technicalities of the sales contract and handover can bring disaster.

In many cases, the seller and buyer keep their regular attorneys throughout the closing process. However, some people decide to save some money and complexity by hiring one lawyer to handle the sale, an unbiased expert who will represent both parties fairly.

Either way, have your attorney on speed dial as you work through the final deal-making.

Initial Work

In order to close the sale, you have to agree with the buyer on several key points and take care of a few important issues:

- **Final Price:** Due diligence will probably have put downward pressure on price.
- **Price Allocation:** Exactly how the price is allocated is an important part of the negotiation.

- **Closing Date:** This is not just important for planning a celebration. Certain regular and ongoing expenses, such as payroll, rent, and utilities, will have to be prorated. For this reason, a closing date at the end of a month or the end of a pay period is usually easiest.

- **Buyer's Concerns:** The buyer may have laid out specific concerns in his Letter of Intent and raised new ones during due diligence. It's necessary to address all of these adequately before closing.

- **Loan Documents:** If you are financing the deal, you'll need a solid agreement that spells out all the terms.

- **Transfers:** You must arrange for the transfer of all titles, leases, and other transferable contracts included in the sale.

- **Settlement Sheet:** This is a final accounting of the deal with adjustments for legal fees, commissions and other expenses related to the closing.

As you work through these, remind yourself again to keep the momentum going. Avoid delays and remember that you both want to get a deal done. Once you've dealt with these issues, you're ready for the drafting of the sales contract.

The Sales Contract

The sales contract is the document that sets out all the details of the sale and the handover. Expect there to be some continuing negotiation over some of the details and the wording of this agreement.

The length of the sales contract depends on the size and complexity of your business and its sale, but most are between 10 and 25 pages.

You can find sales contract templates online and buy software that saves you thousands of dollars in legal fees, but these are usually very vague and may not comply with your state and local laws. Don't be afraid to spend the money on having an attorney draft a contract that is comprehensive and legally sound.

Have your attorney draft the initial contract when possible.. The buyer and his attorney will then review and amend the document. This back and forth continues until both parties are satisfied that the contract contains exactly the right terms, provisions, and guarantees.

Although you will be letting your professional team handle the details of the sales contract, it is a good idea to know what it normally includes so you can be prepared for the negotiation or discussion:

- Names of the seller(s) and buyer(s)
- Closing date
- Statement of price and terms
- Assets included in the sale
- Liabilities assumed by the buyer
- Inventory

- Accounts receivable included in the sale
- Allocation of assets
- Statement of absence of participation of brokers or finders
- Indemnification clause
- Business transfer agreements
- Default provisions
- Employee termination clause
- Buyer's representations and warranties
- Seller's representations and warranties
- Attachments (promissory note, consulting or employment contract, non-compete clause, etc.)

Your attorney can guide you through these items, but one of them deserves special attention here: the seller's representations and warranties.

The seller's representations and warranties is a part of the contract that outlines exactly what you are promising to the buyer about the business. It's essential that an attorney draft this properly.

Why are your representations and warranties so important? Throughout the selling process, you have tried to portray your business in the best possible light. Now, in this part of the sales contract, you are saying that you have not misrepresented anything. If you *have* misrepresented things or can be *shown* to have misrepresented things, you might be in trouble. In this situation, a buyer has trouble running the business can try to sue you, and you could be left with nothing.

Here are some of the claims that might appear in your representations:

- You have legal ownership of all assets, both tangible and intangible
- The tangible assets are in good working order
- There are no known liability issues or pending legal actions
- All taxes are up-to-date
- Financial statements are materially accurate

Your representations and warranties are legally binding. You can see now why it is necessary to be completely upfront about negative issues throughout the selling process.

Alright, once the sales contract is acceptable to buyer and seller, you're ready to close.

The Closing

An attorney or escrow agent can handle the closing of your business sale. In most business sales, it is the seller's attorney that does this.

In some, an escrow agent acts as a third party hired to handle the transaction. The agent will guide buyer and seller through the sale, receiving funds from the buyer and ensuring all contingencies have been taken care of before facilitating the signing of the closing documents and releasing the funds to the seller.

If you don't use an escrow agent, then your attorney can handle the closing in his or her office and guide you through the process.

Make sure you check with your attorney to ensure your closing conforms with any local or state bulk sales statutes.

The following people are usually present at the closing "ceremony:"

- The seller(s) and, depending on the state, spouses
- The buyer(s) and, depending on the state, spouses
- Attorney(s)
- Third-party loan guarantor(s)
- Business broker, if used

At the closing, you will need to review and sign some or all of the following:

- Purchase and sales contract
- Settlement sheet
- Loan documents
- Bill of sale
- Non-competition agreement
- Consulting / employment contract
- Lease transfer documents
- Vehicle ownership transfer documents
- Other asset transfer documents

- Other contract transfer documents
- IRS form 8594 (asset acquisition statement)

Once all of this paperwork is taken care of, you can receive your down payment and begin your new life as the non-owner of your former business.

But wait. It's not over.

For starters, it is good form to show your appreciation to the buyer. This could mean a champagne toast or some kind of gift. You've navigated a tough road with this person or these people, and the successful sale of a business is a big accomplishment. Treat it like one.

The Handoff

The buyer knows a lot about the business you have just sold to him, but he's not yet ready to just walk in and run the show. There are certain items that you'll need to hand over immediately. These include:

- Keys to the premises, as well as to any vehicles, cases, and cabinets
- Owner manuals for all equipment and vehicles

There's also certain information that the buyer needs to operate, including:

- Alarm codes
- Computer/software usernames and passwords

- Lists of customers, suppliers, and distributors

And finally, you want the buyer to have your contact information because, even if you are not staying on as an employee or consultant, he might need to contact you. If you financed the deal, you'll want to make sure the buyer knows how to send you money and financial updates.

Winding Down

Once the deal is done, you will have to separate yourself from the different parts of the business. If your business is an LLC or corporation and the sale was not an entity sale, then you'll have to dissolve. This involves holding a meeting, notifying the IRS, and filing articles of dissolution.

Next you'll need to notify:

- Creditors and/or Debtors
- Landlords (Lessors)
- Contracted business associates

You'll also need to cancel or close:

- Permits and licenses
- Bank accounts
- Leases (if not included in sale)
- Credit cards
- Utilities
- Insurance policies

Then you'll need to pay or distribute:

- All bills and liabilities not included in the sale
- Final wages and fees to IRS and other authorities
- Remaining assets to yourself and any partners

And finally, you should file all the necessary tax forms.

The Transition

If you have a consulting or employment contract with the new owner of the business, you will be working with him in the future. Whether you have this arrangement or not, the business, its new owner, and its employees will be going through a challenging transition period. Your assistance, care, and respect through this transition are important. Even if you are not financing the sale, you surely want the business to prosper. And you probably want the employees to maintain a sense of security.

The first and most difficult thing about this transition is the announcement. Who will you tell first? How will you tell people? What will you tell them? These are important questions, and you should plan your announcements carefully.

Here are a few guidelines for announcing the sale of your business:

- From best to worst, the methods of announcement are: in person, by phone, by email, letting someone else do it

- Try not to let key people hear through the grapevine
- Start with the people who have been most crucial to your success
- Explain what the transition looks like
- Reassure people about security and stability
- Introduce the new owner and show confidence in his abilities and plans for the business

Employees are the first group of people you'll want to inform because their morale will have the greatest influence on the future success of the business. Make the announcement to all employees at the same time, if possible. Explain your reasons for selling and ask for their co-operation in the transition and their confidentiality as you make your announcements. Give them a clear timeline and let them know your plans. Their first feeling might be fear that their jobs might not be safe, and their work lives might change for the worse. Reassure them. Arrange to make your announcement with the new owner present and then make your exit to give everyone a chance to chat without you.

Now comes one of the most difficult parts: stepping back. Even if you understand that you no longer own the business, it can be difficult to behave that way. This is especially true if you are staying on to help in the transition. Let the new owner take on your former role, even if his management style is very different from yours. Don't hang around too much. Let the new owner really feel physical ownership over the space, and only offer advice or assistance when he asks you for it. It is usually not a good idea to try to coach employees through the transition too much. Don't even attempt to answer questions about the future except in general positive terms.

If you can, take a vacation. It will help the new buyer grow into his new role. Besides, you deserve it! You are part of a small number of people in society who have the courage, the work ethic, and the smarts to build equity in your own business rather than working for someone else.

Resources & Templates

The following pages contain various resources that you'll find useful as you progress through the process of selling your business.

Action Steps

Figure out your exit strategy

- Give it to kids
- Sell it as an operating business
- Shut the doors and liquidate
- File bankruptcy

If selling, who is the buyer?

- Family members
- Partners
- Employees
- Strategic buyers
- Private equity groups
- Financial buyers

Prepare a deal team to help with transaction

- Accountant
- Lawyer
- Tax advisor
- Appraiser
- Business broker

Get the business ready to sell

- Improve or solidify your lease
- Review other contracts

- Get rid of bad inventory
- Clean up, fix, improve the business

Prepare Financial documents

- Organized and computerized
- Gather 3 years Profit & Loss Statements

Learn what buyers are looking for

- Seller's Discretionary Earnings
- Gross margins
- Accounts receivable
- Ratios
- Debt

Other Documents

- Lease agreement
- Employee and freelancer agreements
- Other Contracts

Choose a Method of Valuation

- Asset based for new businesses or poor performers
- Multiple of earnings for most small businesses

Determine a Price Range

- Value all assets
- Figure out your multiplier
- Use rules of thumb
- View listings of similar businesses
- Start at high side of reasonable

Offer Seller Financing for higher price

- Down payment - The more upfront, the lower the price
- Interest - 6% to 9%
- Amortization Period - 3 to 5 years
- Miscellaneous terms – balloon payment, graduated payments, 1st payment date

Create marketing materials

- Confidential business profile
- Blind profile

Advertise your opportunity

- Write effective ads
- Create confidentiality plan
- Post ads

Respond to buyer inquiries

- Types of prospects

- Tracking inquiries
- Collect confidentiality documents

Screening buyers

- Initial phone call
- Business tour
- Get an offer

Negotiate a deal

- Sale type
- Price and Terms
- What's included
- Asset allocation
- Surviving due diligence
- Be prepared ahead of time
- Follow a process
- Defend your price
- Conduct due diligence on buyer
- Close the deal

Questions to ask your advisors

- What experience do you have helping clients with selling their business?

- Can you provide me with references from other clients that hired you to help them with a business sale?

- What sorts of strategic advice can you provide as I go through the process of selling?

- How do you charge for your services & how often will you bill me for services you provide?

- What can I do to make sure you get all the information you need to give me good advice?

- Are you comfortable helping me understand my options in a potential deal instead of trying to only show me the downside?

- Who else within your firm will be available to help on this transaction?

- How do you prefer we communicate throughout the process?

- How long will it take you to return my phone calls or emails?

- If I hire you to help me, are you open to making your conference room available for me to meet with prospective buyers?

- Can you refer me to other professional advisors that would be a good fit for my deal team?

- What happens if I am unhappy with the services you provide?

Should you use a business broker

Think about the following questions as you decide whether or not you want to use a broker. If you decide you want to talk to a broker, we can refer you to a pre-screened broker in your area. Visit DIYBizSales.com/broker for more information.

- Can you afford to pay 10%-12% or a minimum of $12,000 of the transaction price to the broker at closing?

- Do you have the time and energy to continue to run your business while conducting the sale process?

- Will you be able to create advertising and reach enough prospective buyers?

- Would you prefer to have a broker act as a third party to protect your confidentiality or do you want to control exactly who knows your business is for sale?

- Do you have the time required to respond to all inquiries from interested buyers?

- Will you be able to keep track of all interested buyers and their interest level?

- Can you handle the process of negotiating a fair price and terms for your business?

- Are you able to assemble and manage an attorney and accountant throughout the process?

- Do you want to sell the business on your own or would you prefer to have a broker take care of all the details for you?

Required documents for selling your business

- Tax Returns- previous 3 years
- Income Statement or Profit & Loss Statements – previous 3 years and Year To Date
- Balance Sheet – previous 3 years and current
- Property Lease
- Franchise Agreement
- Vendor and Supplier contracts
- Employee Contracts, agreements, and records
- Equipment leases
- List of assets included in the sale
- Inventory reports

SDE worksheet

Income Statement Items		
Sales		$
Cost of Sales $	minus	$
Operating Expenses $	minus	$
Operating Income	equals	$
Other Income / (Expense)	plus/minus	$
Net Income / Unadjusted Pre-Tax Profit	equals	$
Add-Backs		
Depreciation	plus	$
Amortization	plus	$
Interest on loans to business from all lenders	plus	$
Officer / Owner's salary	plus	$
Payroll: wages, payments or benefits to family members	plus	$
Payroll Other: employee benefits paid to owner	plus	$
Auto for owner's and/or spouse personal use	plus	$
Auto insurance for owner's benefit	plus	$
Auto repairs & maintenance owner's personal use	plus	$
Contributions and donations	plus	$
Fair market rent adjustment	plus/minus	$
Insurance premiums for owner's health, life, etc.	plus	$
Professional services (legal / accounting / tax)	plus	$
Retirement plan contributions	plus	$
Travel, Meals & Entertainment	plus	$
Extraordinary expenses or (income)	plus/minus	$
Other Discretionary Expenses or (income)	plus/minus	$
Seller Discretionary Earnings (SDE)	equals	$

SDE worksheet instructions

Print out a copy of your Profit & Loss statement for the desired year. Use a new worksheet for each year.

Sales – Enter the gross sales amount from your P&L.

Cost of Sales – Enter the cost of sales or cost of goods sold as shown on your P&L.

Operating Expenses – Enter the operating expenses shown on your P&L.

Operating Income – Subtract cost of sales and operating from sales. This gives you operating income. This number may also be shown on your P&L.

Other Income / (Expense) – Insert other income number from your P&L. You may not have this item listed on your P&L.

Net Income / Unadjusted Pre-Tax Profit. – Add other income or subtract other expense from your operating income to get your net income. This number will be shown on your P&L as well.

Add-Backs – Go through your Operating Expenses line by line and look for any discretionary items. Remember that discretionary expenses are items you ran through the business, but a new owner wouldn't necessarily have to spend. Some common examples are listed below. Remember, your can't add items back unless they show up on your P&L as an expense.

Common discretionary expenses

- Interest on any debt the owner carries in the business
- Income taxes paid by the business
- Excess depreciation
- Excessive rent and/or lease payments
- Fair market rent adjustment
- Finance charges / factoring
- Household repairs or services paid for by the company
- Premiums for owner's health, life, and other insurance policies
- Internet service for owner's benefit
- Maid and cleaning services
- Memberships in health clubs, country clubs, etc.
- Non-business shipping and postage costs
- Payroll and employee benefits paid to the owner
- Personal credit cards paid by the business
- Products and services consumed by the owner's family but paid for by the company
- Season tickets
- Any other discretionary expenses that a new owner would not need to cover in order to run the business effectively

Asset worksheet

	Name	Date Purchased	Original Cost	Fair Market Value	Notes
1					
2					
3					
4					
5					
6					
7					
8					
9					
10					
11					
12					
13					
14					
15					
16					
17					
18					
19					
20					
21					
22					
23					
24					
25					
26					
27					
28					
29					
30					
Total Asset Value					

Probable sales price worksheet

		Liquidation Price	Low Selling Price	Probable Selling Price	Listing Price
1	Business Name:				
2	Scenario Based On:				
3	Date:				
4	Fair Market Asset Value:				
5	Cash Flow:				
6	Probable Multiplier Low:				
7	Probable Multiplier High				
8	CASH FLOW				
9	MULTIPLIER				
10	PRICE FROM ASSETS OR MULTIPLIER				
11	STRATEGIC SELLING PRICE				
12	CASH AT CLOSE (DOWN PAYMENT)				
13	PROMISSORY NOTE AMOUNT				
	PROMISSORY NOTE DETAILS				
14	PROMISSORY NOTE AMOUNT				
15	INTEREST RATE				
16	AMORTIZATION TERM (MONTHS)				
17	MONTHLY PAYMENT				
18	ANNUAL PAYMENT				
	BALLOON PAYMENT DETAILS				
19	BALLOON PAYMENT AMOUNT				
20	MONTH THAT PAYMENT IS MADE				
	TOTAL PROCEEDS				
21	CASH AT CLOSE (DOWN PAYMENT)				
22	PROMISSORY NOTE PROCEEDS				
23	BALLOON PROCEEDS				
24	GROSS TOTAL PROCEEDS				
25	ESTIMATED CLOSING COSTS				
26	BROKER FEE				
27	**NET TOTAL PROCEEDS**				
28	RETAINED ACCOUNTS RECEIVABLE				
29	EXCESS INVENTORY				
30	***TOTAL POTENTIAL PROCEEDS***				

Probable sales price instructions

- 1 Business Name:
- 2 Scenario Based On:SDE worksheet source
- 3 Date: Date of analysis
- 4 Fair Market Asset Value: Enter the number from your asset value worksheet
- 5 Cash Flow: Enter the last year's SDE or weighted SDE
- 6 Probable Multiplier Low: Low end of SDE Multiple
- 7 Probable Multiplier High: High end of SDE Multiple
- 8 Cash Flow Same as line 5
- 9 Multiplier: Enter high and low multiplier in high and low columns. Add high and low multiplier and divide by 2 to get average multiplier for probable sale price column
- 10 Price From Assets/Multiplier: Enter asset value from line 4 in liquidation column. Multiply line 8 by line 9 in other columns.
- 11 Strategic Selling Price: Round line 10 up or down to come to an even number.
- 12 Cash At Close (Down Payment): Liquidation gets all cash at close. Low price gets 75% of SDE, Probable gets 100% of SDE, High price gets 135% of SDE cash at close.
- 13 Promissory Note Amount: Subtract Line 12 from Line 11.
- 14 Promissory Note Amount: Same as line 13
- 15 Interest Rate: Enter a value between 5% and 9%
- 16 Amortization Term (Months): Enter a value between 72 and 120 months
- 17 Monthly Payment: Use your calculator or the internet to find the loan payment amounts. Try http://www.bretwhissel.net/amortization/
- 18 Annual Payment: Multiply Line 17 times 12 to get annual payment amount
- 19 Balloon Payment Amount: Use your calculator or the internet to find the balloon payment amounts. Try http://www.bretwhissel.net/amortization/

- 20 Month That Payment Is Made: Balloon payments should be due sometime after the 36th month, but before the 72nd month.
- 21 Cash At Close (Down Payment): Same as line 12
- 22 Promissory Note Proceeds: Multiply Line 17 times the number of payments made to get total note payment amount. Hint:
- number of payments is usually Line 20 minus 1. Ex. If balloon is due in 61st month, you will receive 60 payments.
- 23 Balloon Proceeds: Same as line 19
- 24 Gross Total Proceeds: Add Lines 21, 22, and 23 to get gross proceeds
- 25 Estimated Closing Costs: This covers attorney and escrow fees to prepare and execute proper closing documents. $2,000 is usually a safe amount to budget for this. If unsure, call an attorney and ask.
- 26 Broker Fee: If using a broker, expect to pay 10-12% of the transaction value or $15,000, whichever is greater. Remember that this entire fee is paid at closing.
- 27 Net Total Proceeds: Subtract Line 25 and 26 from Line 24
- 28 Retained Accounts Receivable: If you have any accounts receivable, you will usually not pass them on to a new owner.
- 29 Excess Inventory: If you are carrying excess inventory above and beyond what's needed for normal operations, you can sell it off before bringing your business to market.
- 30 Total Potential Proceeds: Add Lines 27, 28, and 29 to get your total potential proceeds.

Sanity Test

This test helps you figure out if the buyer will have any money left over to pay himself if he buys your business.

The deal won't work if there isn't enough money left over at the end of the month for the buyer to pay himself a fair salary for working in the business.

		Example 1	Example 2
SDE:		$75,000	$75,000
Sales Price:		$225,000	$375,000
Annual Debt Service assuming 100k down and remainder financed at @8%:		$18,199	$46,590

		Example 1	Example 2
	SDE	$75,000	$75,000
minus	Annual Debt Service	$18,199	$46,590
equals	Amount left for Owner Salary & Extra Profit	$56,801	$28,410

Example 1 above shows a reasonable price based on a 3x multiple. After making loan payments, he has more than $56,000 left over to pay himself for working in the business full time.

Example 2 shows what happens if the seller tries to charge too much for the business. At a 5x multiple of cash flow, the debt service takes away more than $46,000 of the earnings from the business. This leaves just over $28,000 for the buyer to pay himself for working full time in the business. Do you think that a buyer with the ability to invest $100,000 as a down payment in your business will actually work full time in your business for less than $30,000 per year? Not likely.

Template:

	Seller's Discretionary Earnings	$
minus	Annual Debt Service	$
minus	Return on Cash Investment	$
equals	Amount left for Owner Salary & Extra Profit	$

Business Questionnaire

Company Overview and History

Describe your business and what it does:_____

_____

_____

_____

When was your business founded?_____

When did you acquire the business?_____

How has the business grown since it was founded?_____

_____

_____

Describe any licenses or permits required to operate this business:

_____

_____

What is the legal structure of the business?

(Sole proprietor, partnership, LLC, S-corp, C-corp)_____

_____

Who are the current owners and what percentage does each own?_____

Product and/or Service Overview

Describe your products and/or services:_____

_____

_____

_____

_____

Sales and Marketing

Describe your sales and marketing process:_____

_____

_____

_____

_____

What is your website address?_____

What kind of advertising do you use and what does it cost?_____

_____

_____

Business Strengths

What does your business do better than its competitors? (strengths)

_____

_____

_____

_____

Growth Opportunities

What do its competitors do better than your business? (weaknesses)

_____

_____

_____

_____

_____

How could a new owner turn these weaknesses into strengths?___

_____

_____

_____

_____

Any other attractive things about your business that buyer should know?_____

_____

_____

Location and Facility Summary

What is the business address?_____

_____

Square footage:_____

Lease cost per month:_____

Are you responsible for paying taxes, common area maintenance or other fees associated with the lease?_____

_____

Is there any real estate included in the sale?_____

_____

_____

_____

Briefly describe the building:_____

_____

_____

_____

Briefly describe the neighborhood:_____

_____

_____

_____

Employee Information

Do you actively work in the business?_____

Describe your involvement in the business operations:_____

_____

_____

List your employees, their hourly rate, hours worked per week, and tenure.

1._____

2._____

3._____

4._____

5._____

6._____

7._____

8._____

9._____

10._____

Competitor & Industry Information

Describe any industry trends:_____

_____

_____

_____

Why is this a good industry to be in?_____

_____

_____

_____

Why is this business better than the local competitors? _____

_____

_____

_____

Transition

How many hours of transition time are included in the sale?_____

How long does the buyer have to use these hours?

_____

Will you be available for additional hours for an extra fee?_____

If so, what is the hourly rate?_____

Price and Terms

What is the price of your business?_____

What is the minimum down payment required?_____

_____

What is the interest rate and other terms for any seller
financing?_____

_____

_____

What are the minimum requirements for a buyer to qualify for
seller financing?_____

_____

_____

Are you willing to enter a non-compete agreement?_____

_____

If so, what are the terms?_____

_____

_____

Financial Summary

Year	20__	20__	20__
Revenue	$	$	$
SDE	$	$	$

Attachments

At the end of your profile, you can attach any documents that would help the buyer learn more about your business and the industry. Here's a list of examples:

- Brochures
- Product information
- Press clippings
- Industry analysis
- Asset list
- Photographs

List of sites and places to advertise

Site Name	Price
Acquireo.com	49.95-89.95 one time
Bestbusinessesforsaleonly.com	29.95-59.95 per month
Bizben.com	30.00-45.00 per month
Bizbuysell.com	69.95-99.95 per month
Bizhwy.com	14.95 per 60 days
Bizlinkin.com	9.95-19.95 per month
Bizquest.com	69.95-99.95 per month
Biztrader.com	59.00 until sold
Businessbroker.net	99.95 2 month listing
Businessnation.com	30.00 per month
Businessbrokerjournal.com	49.95 per month
Businessesforsale.com	89.00 per month
Businessmart.com	35.99 per month
Buybusiness.com	12.00-26.00 per month
Craigslist.org	FREE
Globalbx.com	FREE
Mergerplace.com	39.95-79.95 for 120 days

*Note- these sites were gathered in February 2011 via an Internet search.
The publishers don't endorse any of these sites

Buyer questionnaire

Name:_____

Phone Number:_____

Email:_____

Source:_____

Mailing Address:_____

_____

Why are you interested in buying a business?

_____

_____

_____

What made you interested in this business?

_____

_____

_____

How long have you been looking?

_____

Owned a business before?_____

Purchased a business before?_____

Describe your relevant work experience.

_____

_____

_____

Describe your relevant education.

_____

_____

_____

How do you plan to finance the purchase?

_____

_____

_____

Who else will be involved in your decision to buy?

_____

_____

_____

Deal flowchart

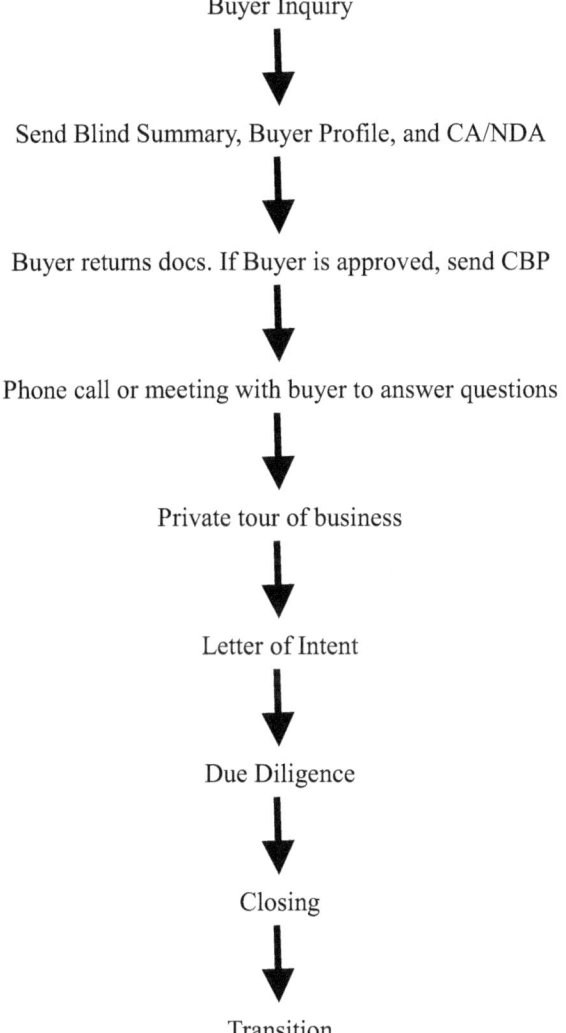

Buyer Inquiry

Send Blind Summary, Buyer Profile, and CA/NDA

Buyer returns docs. If Buyer is approved, send CBP

Phone call or meeting with buyer to answer questions

Private tour of business

Letter of Intent

Due Diligence

Closing

Transition

Buyer tracking worksheet

Name:_____

Phone:_____

Email:_____

Notes: _____

_____

Inquiry Date:_____

Notes: _____

_____

CA Date:_____

Notes: _____

_____

Meeting Date:_____

Notes: _____

_____

Tour Date:_____

Notes:_____

_____

Conversation Log:

Due diligence checklist

The following list contains some of the common items that a buyer may request during due diligence. Buyer may not ask for all of these or may in fact ask for items not listed here.

Be smart with disclosure. It is OK to deny, hold back, or change some requests. For example, customer lists can be provided to the buyer on the morning of closing. Talk to your lawyer and account for specific due diligence advice.

- Organizational chart.
- List of owners and percentage of ownership.
- A Certificate of Good Standing from the Secretary of State.
- A list of all of assumed names.
- Financial statements for past three years.
- List of all debts and liabilities.
- List of inventory.
- List of accounts receivable.
- List of accounts payable.
- A description of depreciation and amortization over the past five years.
- List of fixed assets and the locations thereof.
- All U.C.C. filings.
- All leases of equipment.
- List of sales and purchases of major equipment during last three years.
- Copies of all real estate leases, deeds, mortgages, title policies, surveys, variances or use permits.

- List of intellectual property, including patents, trademarks and copyrights.

- A description of important technical know-how.

- A description of methods used to protect trade secrets and know-how.

- Any "work for hire" agreements.

- A schedule and copies of all consulting agreements.

- A list of employees including positions, current salaries, and years of service.

- All employment, consulting, nondisclosure, nonsolicitation or noncompetition agreements between the Company and any of its employees.

- Resumés of key employees.

- The Company's personnel handbook and List of all employee benefits and holiday, vacation, and sick leave policies.

- Summary plan descriptions of qualified and non-qualified retirement plans.

- A description of worker's compensation claim history.

- A description of unemployment insurance claims history.

- Copies of any governmental licenses, permits or consents.

- Any correspondence or documents relating to any proceedings of any regulatory agency.

- A listing of hazardous substances used in the Company's operations.

- Federal and State income tax returns for the last three years.

- States sales tax returns for the last three years.

- Employment tax filings for three years.

- All security agreements and guaranties to which the Company is a party.

- Any installment sale agreements.

- Any distribution agreements, sales representative agreements, marketing agreements, and supply agreements.

- The Company's standard quote, purchase order, invoice and warranty forms.

- All nondisclosure or noncompetition agreements to which the Company is a party.

- All other material contracts.

- A list of all existing products or services.

- List of the Company's twelve largest customers in terms of sales thereto and a description of sales thereto over a period of two years.

- Any supply or service agreements.

- List of unfilled orders.

- A list and explanation for any major customers lost over the last two years.

- The Company's current advertising plan/budgets, and printed marketing materials.

- A description of the Company's major competitors.

- List of all pending or threatened litigation.

- Copies of insurance policies possibly providing coverage as to pending or threatened litigation.

- Copies of the Company's general liability, personal and real property, product liability, errors and omissions, key-man, directors and officers, worker's compensation, and other insurance.

- List of the Company's insurance claims history for past three years.

- List of all law firms, accounting firms, consulting firms, and similar professionals engaged by the Company during past five years.

- Copies of all articles and press releases relating to the Company within the past three years. .

List of closing documents

The following list shows a sampling of documents that may be required to transfer your business to a new owner.

These documents should always be prepared by an attorney. Be smart, don't download them from the internet and try to edit to serve your purposes.

Many times, sellers and buyers can split the cost of hiring a neutral closing attorney to draft these documents and conduct the closing.

- Asset Purchase Agreement
- Promissory Note
- Security Agreement
- UCC-1 Financing Statement
- Personal Guaranty
- Bill of Sale
- Corporate Resolution – Seller
- Corporate Resolution – Buyer
- Consent to Use of Name
- Lease Assignment/Agreement
- Franchise transfer agreement

Pete's Pets
Case Study

Pete owns a small pet store in a suburban strip mall. He's worked in the store since he opened it 10 years ago. Now it's time for him to sell it and move on to something new.

This example will show you the following items needed to get the business ready to sell:

- Original profit and loss statement
- SDE worksheet
- Sales price and terms worksheet
- Business Questionnaire
- Confidential business profile
- Blind Profile
- Web advertisements

Sample P&L Statement

Pete's Pets
Profit & Loss Statement

	Year		
	20x1	**20x2**	**20x3**
Income			
Sales	$365,000	$358,000	$372,000
Services	$0	$0	$0
Other Income	$0	$0	$0
Total Income	$365,000	$358,000	$372,000
Cost of Sales / Cost of Goods Sold	$197,000	$184,000	$193,000
Gross Income	$168,000	$174,000	$179,000
Expenses			
Advertising	$8,350	$7,500	$6,200
Bank Service Charges	$962	$984	$1,107
Depreciation	$500	$500	$500
Insurance	$1,221	$1,202	$1,121
Interest	$2,402	$2,402	$2,402
Miscellaneous Expense	$8,500	$2,200	$5,734
Motor Vehicle	$3,800	$3,600	$3,250
Office Supplies	$962	$908	$876
Postage & Printing	$125	$105	$98
Professional Expenses	$2,500	$2,400	$2,600
Rent	$24,000	$24,000	$24,000
Repairs & Maintenance	$1,082	$1,156	$1,017
Subscriptions	$250	$187	$213
Telephone	$3,200	$2,850	$2,987
Training, Seminars and Travel	$980	$2,600	$1,200
Utilities	$3,945	$3,945	$3,945
Wages & Salaries	$83,500	$92,500	$89,600
Total Expenses	$146,279	$149,038	$146,850
Profit / (Loss)	**$21,721**	**$24,962**	**$32,150**

Seller Discretionary Earnings Worksheet

Pete's Pets
Seller's Discretionary Earnings Worksheet

Income Statement Items		20_X1	20_X2	20_X3
Sales		$365,000	$358,000	$372,000
Cost of Sales $	minus	$197,000	$184,000	$193,000
Operating Expenses $	minus	$146,279	$149,038	$146,850
Net Income	equals	$21,721	$24,962	$32,150
Add-Backs				
Depreciation	plus	$2,835	$2,538	$2,387
Amortization	plus	$0	$0	$0
Interest on loans to business from all lenders	plus	$2,402	$2,402	$2,402
Officer / Owner's salary	plus	$42,000	$42,000	$42,000
Payroll and Benefits to Family	plus	$0	$0	$0
Payroll Other: employee benefits paid to owner	plus	$0	$0	$0
Auto for owner's and/or spouse personal use	plus	$2,800	$2,800	$2,800
Auto insurance for owner's benefit	plus	$1,200	$1,200	$1,200
Auto repairs & maintenance owner's personal use	plus	$0	$0	$0
Contributions and donations	plus	$0	$0	$0
Fair market rent adjustment	plus/minus	$0	$0	$0
Insurance premiums for owner's health, life, etc.	plus	$0	$0	$0
Professional services (legal / accounting / tax)	plus	$500	$500	$500
Retirement plan contributions	plus	$0	$0	$0
Travel, Meals & Entertainment	plus	$0	$0	$0
Extraordinary expenses or (income)	plus/minus	$0	$0	$0
Other Discretionary Expenses or (income)	plus/minus	$0	$0	$0
Seller Discretionary Earnings (SDE)	equals	$73,458	$76,402	$83,439

Value Scenario Worksheet

Business Name:	Pete's Pets			
Scenario Based On:	Owner Provided Cash Flow Estimate			
Date:				
Fair Market Asset Value:	$81,575			
Cash Flow:	$77,766			
Probable Multiplier Low:	2.00			
Probable Multiplier High	3.00			

	Liquidation Price	Low Selling Price	Probable Selling Price	Listing Price
CASH FLOW		$77,766	$77,766	$77,766
MULTIPLIER		2.00	2.50	3.00
PRICE FROM ASSETS OR MULTIPLIER	$81,575	$155,532	$194,415	$233,298
STRATEGIC SELLING PRICE	$80,000	$155,000	$195,000	$235,000
CASH AT CLOSE (DOWN PAYMENT)	$80,000	$60,000	$80,000	$105,000
PROMISSORY NOTE AMOUNT		$95,000	$115,000	$130,000
PROMISSORY NOTE DETAILS				
PROMISSORY NOTE AMOUNT		$95,000	$115,000	$130,000
INTEREST RATE		8.00%	8.00%	8.00%
AMORTIZATION TERM (MONTHS)		120	120	120
MONTHLY PAYMENT		$1,153	$1,395	$1,577
ANNUAL PAYMENT		$13,831	$16,743	$18,927
BALLOON PAYMENT DETAILS				
BALLOON PAYMENT AMOUNT		$56,845	$68,812	$77,788
MONTH THAT PAYMENT IS MADE		61	61	61
TOTAL PROCEEDS				
CASH AT CLOSE (DOWN PAYMENT)	$80,000	$60,000	$80,000	$105,000
PROMISSORY NOTE PROCEEDS		$69,157	$83,716	$94,636
BALLOON PROCEEDS		$56,845	$68,812	$77,788
GROSS TOTAL PROCEEDS	$80,000	$186,002	$232,528	$277,423
ESTIMATED CLOSING COSTS	$2,000	$2,000	$2,000	$2,000
NET TOTAL PROCEEDS	$78,000	$184,002	$230,528	$275,423
RETAINED ACCOUNTS RECEIVABLE	$0	$0	$0	$0
EXCESS INVENTORY	$0	$0	$0	$0
TOTAL POTENTIAL PROCEEDS	*$78,000*	*$184,002*	*$230,528*	*$275,423*
BROKER FEE	$12,000	$15,500	$19,500	$23,500
TOTAL PROCEEDS WITH BROKER	$66,000	$168,502	$211,028	$251,923

Final Price And Terms

Based on the value scenario worksheet, Pete's Pets will likely sell for between $155,000 and $235,000.

Pete should consider advertising his business for sale at $235,000, and offering seller financing of $130,000 of the purchase price.

Business Questionnaire

Company Overview and History

Describe your business and what it does:

Retailer of pets and pet related supplies. Sell quality made in America products and only sell animals from reputable breeders.

When was your business founded?

2000

When did you acquire the business?

N/a...I started it in 2000

How has the business grown since it was founded?

Started off slowly, but we built a reputation for great customer service. Added a website with ecommerce in 2005, but haven't done a lot with it.

Business Strengths

What does your business do better than its competitors? (strengths)

Excellent customer service, with knowledgeable sales staff

Locally owned, not a chain store

Better products

Cleaner more appealing

Any other attractive things about your business that buyer should know?

Very fun business to run, customers are great

Growth Opportunities

What do its competitors do better than your business? (weaknesses)

Utilize ecommerce

Offer other services – grooming, training

Keep better hours...we are closed on Sundays and Mondays

Collect customer info via coupons, buyers club, etc

How could a new owner turn these weaknesses into strengths?

Upgrade website, hire manager for Sunday and Monday, form partnerships with other service providers or offer other service

Product and/or Service Overview

Describe your products and/or services:

We only sell pets from certified breeders, not from puppy mills or other similar type outfits

Wherever possible, we sell locally made and sourced foods, treats and accessories. We don't carry the big national brands because it is too tough to be competitive with big box stores

Sales and Marketing

Describe your sales and marketing process:

We greet customers as they come in and use questions to find out what they are looking for. We offer helpful solutions and offer add-on products where appropriate

What is your website address?

WWW.DOMAIN.COM

What kind of advertising do you use and what does it cost?

Yellow pages 100/mo, newspaper $300/mo, youth sports $500/mo

Location and Facility Summary

What is the business address?

1234 MAIN STREET, ANYTOWN, USA

Square footage:

1200

Lease cost per month:

2500

Are you responsible for paying taxes, common area maintenance or other fees associated with the lease?

Yes...included in 2500 cost

Is there any real estate included in the sale?

No

Briefly describe the building:

Modern suburban strip mall built in 2010 anchored by large grocery store

Briefly describe the neighborhood:

Affluent suburb, high household income

Competitor & Industry Information

Describe any industry trends:

Steady growth, slow economy hasn't really hurt the business

Why is this a good industry to be in?

People always like to pamper their pets. The recent quality issues of foreign pet food helped us keep customers

Who are your top competitors?

Pet smart

Walmart

Petco

Online

Why is this business better than the local competitors?

We offer better products and can help people solve problems.

Operational Information

What are your hours of operation?

11am to 8pm Tuesday through Saturday

Do you actively work in the business?

YES

Describe your involvement in the business operations:

Work in the business full time, 5 days per week

List your employees, their hourly rate, hours worked per week, and tenure.

Alice, 8/hr, 10hrs/wk, 4 yrs

Bob, 10/hr, 20hrs/wk, 1 yr

Chris, 10/hr, 20 hrs/wk, 6 yrs

Describe any licenses or permits required to operate this business:

State sales tax license

What is the legal structure of the business?

(Sole proprietor, partnership, LLC, S-corp, C-corp)

LLC

Who are the current owners and what percentage does each own?

PETE PAULSEN 100%

Transition

How many hours of transition time are included in the sale?

80

How long does the buyer have to use these hours?

90 DAYS

Will you be available for additional hours for an extra fee?

YES

If so, what is the hourly rate?

20/HR

Price and Terms

What is the price of your business?

235,000

What is the minimum down payment required?

105,000

What is the interest rate and other terms for any seller financing?

8% interest, amortized over 120 months with balloon payment due in 61st month.

What are the minimum requirements for a buyer to qualify for seller financing?

All seller financing subject to seller's approval of buyers financial and credit history.

Are you willing to enter a non-compete agreement?

Yes.

If so, what are the terms?

3 years from sale and 15 miles from store.

Give a brief description and market value of Furniture Fixtures and Equipment that are included in the sale price.

Various equipment related to the pet store. Market value of $41,575.

How much inventory is included in the sale price?

$40,000. Final inventory amount to be adjusted at closing.

Financial Summary

Year	20X1	20X2	20X3
Revenue	$365,000	$342,000	$357,000
SDE	$73,458	$76,402	$83,439

Business profile

Pete's Pets

Confidential Business Profile

Company Overview and History

Pete's Pets

123 Main Street

Anytown, USA, ZIP

Asking Price: $235,000

Pete's Pets is a retailer of pets and pet related supplies. They take pride in selling quality products that are made in America, and they make sure to only sell animals from reputable breeders. Pete's Pets makes sure only to offer their customers the very best available in terms of quality.

Pete's Pets was founded in 2000. Their dedication to providing customers with a superior product accompanied with great customer service has helped them build a very positive reputation for themselves and they have an incredibly loyal customer base. They also have a website with e-commerce that opened in 2005.

Business Strengths & Attributes

• Pete's Pets prides itself on offering superior customer service. At a chain store service is impersonal and oftentimes non-existent, but the atmosphere at Pete's allows customers a more attentive shopping environment.

• The sales staff is not only attentive, but also very knowledgeable. All are previous pet owners, and the staff here can answer any pet-related question or at least know how to research the answer.

• The store is locally owned, and not a chain. Thus, it holds community ties. Due to recent stigmas attached to the chain store shopping experience, the public has recently taken more interest in local small business and are much more supportive to the Mom & Pop type stores in the neighborhood.

• The products offered at Pete's Pets are American-made. A recent quality control issue concerning pet food manufactured overseas has made customers rethink their purchases. Domestically made products are hot on the market because they are held to higher standards of quality and they help build the local economy.

• Pete's Pets puts special emphasis on the appearance and cleanliness of their stores; customers have commented on the pleasant environment. Many pet stores remind customers of their business with the disagreeable smells, but Pete's Pets is clean and well ventilated.

• The owner says that the business is very enjoyable to run for somebody that is passionate about pets, and that he likes working with the customers who are friend local to the community.

Growth Opportunities

Pete's Pets is a strong pet retailer with significant opportunities for a new owner to grow the business. While Pete's does have a professionally designed website, there is room to improve it and make it more profitable. The site has ecommerce capabilities, but needs more traffic. Better internet marketing and search engine optimization could bring in a new stream of revenue from internet shoppers. The business also has enough extra space to start offering additional services. Connecting a grooming service or a pet training school to Pete's Pets would draw in new customers, as well as providing the regular customers with new options. It also lends the opportunity to network with other local service providers.

Pete's Pets is currently closed on Sundays and Mondays; operating during these days would generate more profit. This option would likely require hiring and/or training additional staff to run the store, but the long-term profit will likely outweigh the initial cost. Current customers would be pleased with more availability and potential new customers that run errands on these days would be attracted to Pete's.

Pete's Pets would benefit from collecting customer information via surveys and providing coupons, a buyer's club and other such initiatives to draw in extra business. A coupon service would provide customers with more incentive to shop at the store, while also providing the business with an opportunity to remain in consistent contact with the customer. Coupon books received in the mail, e-mail deals, newsletters, and special promotions all have the potential to increase revenue at Pete's Pets.

Products and Services

Pete's Pets only sells pets from certified breeders, following the highest standards of animal care. Puppy mills and similar sources are an insult to their ethics and would never be pursued as a way to acquire new animals. The pets at Pete's are healthy and well treated so they're ready to go home and love the first family that wants them. Pete's also sells only local, American-made supplies. At Pete's they believe in high quality products, which means getting them from trusted sources. The national economy is suffering due to outsourcing and chain stores. Pete's Pets makes an effort to fight these obstacles by supporting the local economy.

Sales and Marketing

The biggest draw of Pete's Pets is the individual attention given to each customer. Every customer is greeted when they enter the store in order to present a welcoming atmosphere. The staff then continues to ask the customer questions, in a friendly manner, to establish their pet needs. This ensures that every person entering the store has the best possible shopping experience.

Their website is www.domain.com, though it could benefit from some improvements as previously suggested. Pete's Pets also utilizes different forms of print advertising. They have a consistent advertisement in the Yellow Pages, which runs $100/month. They also take advantage of their local ties by advertising in local newspapers, at $300/month. Their final form of marketing is through sponsoring youth sports. This is the most costly method, but also the most meaningful. Pete's Pets has established its place in the community once again with their generous commitment to children's well being, totaling $500/month. The overall costs of print advertising are low compared to the amount of visibility for the name of Pete's Pets and the fond ties that the community feels for the business.

Location and Facilities

Pete's Pets can easily be found at their charming location in Anytown, USA.

•   The store is located in an affluent suburb with a high household income. Store size is approximately 1200 square feet.

•   The monthly lease amount is $2500. This includes taxes, common area maintenance, and all fees associated with the property.

•   Pete's Pets is located in a modern suburban strip mall that was built in 2010 and is anchored by a large grocery store.

Industry Overview

Current industry trends show steady growth in the market of pet supplies. The slow economy has had little impact on the business at Pete's Pets. Even in hard times, most pet owners view the pets as family and will not ignore their basic needs or even reduce their pampering and play. In addition, recent issues with foreign pet products have also had a positive impact on Pete's Pets. When details of poorly made or dangerous pet products made abroad were revealed, Pete's Pets absorbed many new customers due to their shared loyalty to American-made products.

Competitors

Pete's Pets' top competitors include PetSmart, WalMart, Petco, and online retailers. This is likely due to prices and convenience of hours of operation, online service and locale.

Store Hours

Pete's Pets is open Tuesday – Saturday, 11am-8pm. They are currently closed Sunday and Monday. The owner takes an active role in running the business and works at the shop full time.

Employee Chart

Below is a list of the employees who work regularly for this business:

NAME	RATE	WEEKLY HOURS	TENURE
Alice	$8/hr	10	4 years
Bob	$10/hr	20	1 year
Chris	$10/hr	20	6 years

Licenses and Permits

A state sales tax license is required to operate this business, which operates under an LLC legal structure.

Ownership

Pete's Pets is solely owned by Pete Paulsen.

Reason For Selling

Retirement

Transition

The transition period will allow 80 hours with the previous owner. These 80 hours must be redeemed within 90 days of the sale, and any additional transitional help from owner will cost $20/hr.

Asking Price

The asking price for this business is $235,000.

Terms

For qualified buyers, the seller is open to providing seller financing. Any financing is subject to seller's approval of buyer's financial and credit history.

The seller's proposed terms are as follows:

- Minimum down payment: $105,000

- Seller Financing: $130,000

- Interest rate: 8%

- Monthly Payment: $1,577

- Amortized over 120 months

- Balloon payment due in 61st month

Non Compete

The seller is willing to enter into a non-compete agreement. The terms of the agreement cover a 15-mile radius of the location and span a 3 year period.

Furniture, Fixtures and Equipment

The existing furniture, fixtures and equipment within the store and included in the sale is worth approximately $41,575.

Inventory

The sales price includes $40,000 of inventory. The final purchase will be adjusted up or down to reflect actual closing inventory.

Financial Summary

Year	20_X1_	20_X2_	20_X3_
Revenue	$365,000	$342,000	$357,000
SDE	$ 73,458	$ 76,402	$ 83,439

Blind Profile

Remember, the blind profile is a one page advertising document that gives more detail than your web ads, but does not disclose the name or location of your business.

The blind profile contains boiled down portions of your CBP, including:

- Asking Price

- Overview of your business

- Three to five summary points

- Your revenue/earnings table

- Contact info

You may want to include your Confidentiality Agreement/Non-Disclosure Agreement and Buyer Questionnaire to the back of your blind profile so prospective buyers and easily send these docs back if they want more information.

Profitable Pet Store for Sale – With Seller Financing

Price: $235,000
Revenue: $357,000
Cash Flow: $83,439

A small, locally-owned pet company located in suburban Anytown that focuses on retail pets and pet supplies. Business specializes in local, American-made products and tries to focus on the pet-owner demographic that values quality over quantity. They do not carry products made by large chain brands, in general, finding them to be of lower quality.

In addition to pet supplies business also sells dogs, but only from reputable breeders; business does not buy from "puppy mills" and other such institutions. This business has been in existence for nearly ten years, and currently runs on a staff of three part time workers (one at 10 hours per week, the other two at 20), and the owner who works full time.

This business went online with 2005, but the owner hasn't developed ecommerce very much and its web presence remains minimal. Store get most of its business through word of mouth, and has placed a keen emphasis on quality customer service in order to draw more customers in.

The business is located in a suburban strip mall anchored by a grocery store in a relatively well off neighborhood. The owner has found the business a joy to run and working with customers is an enjoyable aspect of running the store, as the clientele is somewhat selective. However, despite the fact that the economy has worsened in recent years, the downturn has affected this business minimally.

Highlights

- Independent store
- Sells higher priced, quality goods with an emphasis on locally made products
- Generating consistent revenue even through the economic downturn

Revenue/Earnings Summary

Year	20_X1_	20_X2_	20_X3_
Revenue	$365,000	$342,000	$357,000
SDE	$73,458	$76,402	$83,439

Contact 123-456-7890 or seller@domain.com for more information

Web Ads

Headline options:

- Independent Pet Store For Sale In Anytown – Seller Financing

- Profitable Pet Store On The Market – Seller Financing

Very successful independent pet store for sale. Low lease costs and reliable business even in time of economic downturn. Three part time employees but open to expansion should new owner seek to extend hours of operation. Consistently produces revenue of $340,000+ yearly. Only competition in area from larger chains, and many customers are seeking a more personal shopping experience for their pet. Seller financing available for qualified buyers.

Have any questions or feedback about the guidebook?

We'd love to hear it.

Visit us online at www.diybizsales.com and send us your thoughts.

.

DISCLAIMER

The business value and transaction information presented on DIYBizSales.com and in this guidebook is designed as a self-help research tool for independent use only. All calculator, worksheets and formulaic results are hypothetical and for illustrative and/or example purposes only. The information provided herein is not intended to provide investment advice, or provide a firm business valuation, or replace an independent business appraisal provided by a qualified business valuation professional in your market or area. We strongly recommend you consult professional business advisors including Attorneys, CPA's, Financial Advisors, Certified Business Appraisers, and Tax Advisors before making any financial or investment decisions. The authors and publishers put together this educational and informative guidebook for your convenience only and do not represent you in an agency, legal, or other role.

The DIYBizSales.com website, this guidebook and the material and information contained within are provided to you on an "as is" basis without any warranties of any kind. In no event shall Launch Innovations Group, LLC, its employees, agents, owners, or affiliates be liable for any direct, indirect, incidental, punitive, or consequential damages of any kind whatsoever with respect to this service, services, the information, and the products.